Hawaiian Hiking Trails

The Guide for All the Islands

including Hawaii, Maui, Lanai, Molokai, Oahu and Kauai

Craig Chisholm

The Fernglen Press
473 Sixth Street
Lake Oswego, Oregon 97034

Printed by Lynx Communications Inc., Salem, Oregon
Printed in the United States of America

Distributed in the United Kingdom by Cordee, Leicester, U.K.
Japanese language edition published by Bronze Publishing, Tokyo, Japan.

Library of Congress Cataloging-in-Publication Data

Chisholm, Craig (Craig McRae)
Hawaiian Hiking Trails: The Guide for All the Islands /
  Craig Chisholm. -- Ninth Edition
152 p.: maps, drawings, and photos (some in color)
Includes Index

ISBN 0-9612630-8-3

1. Hiking--Hawaii--Guidebooks.
2. Trails--Hawaii--Guidebooks.
3. Hawaii--Guidebooks.
I. Title
GV199.42.H3C47 1999
919.9604'4--dc21

                                                          98-54249
                                                             CIP

Sunset at Pu'uhonua-o-Honaunau

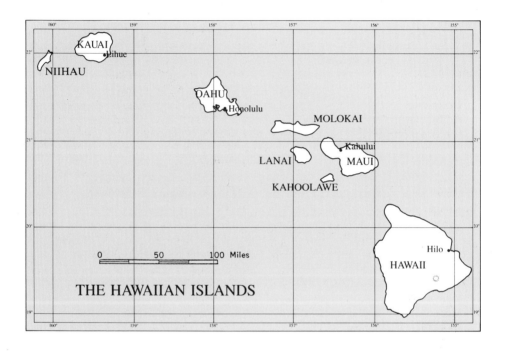

THE HAWAIIAN ISLANDS

0 50 100 Miles

160° 159° 158° 157° 156° 155°

22° KAUAI Lihue
NIIHAU

OAHU Honolulu
MOLOKAI
21° Kahului
LANAI MAUI
KAHOOLAWE

20°
Hilo
HAWAII

19°

Contents

● easiest	● easier	● harder	● hardest

Pahoehoe lava – Hawaii Volcanoes National Park

Tree molds – Mauna Loa in the background   *Akaka Falls – Hawaii*

Ohia and fern forest – Kilauea Iki Trail   *Near Akaka Falls*

Na Pali Coast – Kauai

Spring on Mauna Loa

Ohia lehua blossoms

Ohelo berries

Cinder cone—devastation and regeneration

Hiking high above the helicopters at the end of the Awaawapuhi Trail – Kauai

Halemauu Trail – Haleakala Crater, Maui

Silversword and evening primrose – Haleakala Crater

Hanakapiai Falls – Kauai

Amaumau fern (sadleria) along Halemauu Trail – Maui

Waimea Canyon – Kauai

Kalaupapa Peninsula – a classic shield volcano, Molokai

Garden of the Gods – Lanai

White sand, seashells and coral – Polihua Beach, Lanai

In memory of
Dr. Douglas Murray Burns
Wise teacher and friend of my youth

Preface

Hawaii's landscape changes rapidly. In the decades spanning the various editions of this book, trails have been obliterated by erosion and encroaching vegetation, submerged by earthquakes and tidal waves, or covered by lava. Even the type of vegetation in many areas has changed, with endemic plants disappearing in the face of aggressive newcomers.

The book has once again been revised and updated. The selection of trails has been improved upon, and portions of the book have been rearranged for greater clarity. Maps have been redrawn or amended accordingly and many of the photos have been replaced to better illustrate the trail descriptions.

I gratefully acknowledge the assistance of the personnel of the Hawaii Department of Land and Natural Resources and the National Park Service, the good friends in the Hawaiian Trail and Mountain Club, the Nature Conservancy of Hawaii, the Sierra Club, and others who have generously continued to provide information and advice.

In a larger sense, all of us should be grateful to those who have worked over the years to develop and preserve the trails in the Hawaiian Islands. Various agencies, organizations, and individuals are achieving much. The trail complex on Mount Tantalus, passage of needed legislation, and the development on Na Ala Hele, the Hawai'i Trail and Access System, are among the examples of progress. Through such accomplishments, the public is able to enjoy the trails and learn to value nature in Hawaii, which is the foundation of its preservation.

Chuck Hurst, at Lynx Communications, has shown considerable understanding in our sometimes-arduous transition through various editions from the mechanical pre-press methods of the pre-computer age to the hands-on design capabilities offered by desktop publishing software.

The graphic design and production of this edition was accomplished by my loving and deadline-enforcing wife, Eila, and our son, Kari, who knows how to make the magic inside the machine work.

The ongoing improvement of each edition of Hawaiian Hiking Trails has been the result of Eila's determination, skill and hard work. As my hiking partner, editor, and publisher, she has been invaluable.

Finally, I thank the many hikers who have taken this book on their adventures and enjoyed exploring the beauty of the Hawaiian Islands.

Craig Chisholm

Edited by
Eila Chisholm

Photography by
Eila and Craig Chisholm
Colin Chisholm, front cover photo
Ray Atkeson, back cover (Kauai)
Jeff Dunn, page 39
Sandra Stallcup, page 49
Ellen Schroeder, page 103
Herbert Warner, page 109

Cover Design by
Kari Chisholm

Drawings by
Ellen Schroeder

Maps
Courtesy of U.S. Geological Survey

Use of the Book

A map of all the Hawaiian Islands is in the beginning of the book. The introduction to each island section has an island map on which the areas of the individual trail maps are outlined and identified by number.

The trail descriptions begin with a statistical summary and also include a map and photographs. In the summary, the length of time given for the hike is based on estimated total hiking time for an average hiker. The calories given are what an average hiker would burn up for the complete hike. The trails are rated easiest, easier, harder, and hardest. Though this gives some notion of the relative difficulty of the trails, such ratings are, of course, quite subjective. What is hard for one hiker may be easy for another. Each hiker must judge his or her own capabilities and not go beyond them.

Mileage is given for the entire hike. In most cases this is out and back, except where the trail is ordinarily hiked only in one direction. The highest and lowest elevations reached on the trail are shown to give an idea of the physical exertion required for the hike. As some trails have many ups and downs between the highest and lowest points, the topographical map in the book should be studied to gain the best understanding of the requirements of the trail. The name of agency within whose jurisdiction the trail lies is also included. The agency should be consulted for current information and, for a few trails, permits.

The trail descriptions include overlaid reproductions of portions of U.S. Geological Survey topographical maps. The main trail is marked by a solid black line, the starts of side trails by a single line of dots or dashes, and roadways by double dashed lines. All the maps have true north at the top. Magnetic north lies about 11° northeast of true north. Most maps have 40-foot contour intervals, a few have 50, 80 or 200-foot intervals. Look at the elevations in feet shown on the contours to determine the interval. The maps may have been enlarged or reduced. For approximate scale, reference should be made to the mileage marked on the map along each trail.

Copies of complete topographical maps may be obtained from the U.S. Geological Survey. See the introductory section for address and phone.

The distances, times, routes, and other facts in this book should be considered as estimates only. Descriptions of the trails and other information can at times be subjective and, most important, all conditions can change. This book, though hopefully a useful and generally an accurate aid, must not be relied upon to be always accurate or complete. Hikers are expected to rely on their own experience, preparation, and good on-the-spot judgement for their safety. Consult those in whose jurisdiction a trail lies for current and additional information. Addresses are at the end of the introductory section.

Hiking on the Hawaiian Islands

Many lament the ruin of what once made Hawaii an earthly paradise. Memories are evoked of uncrowded valleys and seashores, now cluttered with highrise dwellings, highways, crowds, and commercialism. Fortunately, this is true only for those who refuse to leave the comfort of their cars. The best of Hawaii still awaits those willing to walk: isolated black-sand beaches, waterfalls cascading into clear pools, valleys dotted with stone ruins, groves of fruit trees planted by long-vanished people, and mountain regions of spectacular beauty.

Many hiking trails lead to these quiet scenes. This book covers a wide selection of the best, described in enough detail to allow the reader to choose suitable trails and areas. The trails included range from pleasant strolls to memorable "character builders." Some fine trails are not described here because of access problems. Too little has been done to assure access to public lands. Hopefully, well-considered planning will improve hiking access to the back country as well as preserve the rights of private landowners.

Climate and Topography

The weather in the Hawaiian Islands varies dramatically from one area to the next but it is remarkably stable the year round in any one place. The constant tradewinds out of the northeast, passing over the rugged terrain, create distinct, almost invariable lines between microclimates. The vastness of the Pacific Ocean moderates the temperature of these trade winds and minimizes seasonal change. The occasional warm, humid Kona winds from the south only occasionally vary this pattern. As the trade winds rise over the mountainous islands, they cool to form clouds which release their moisture, mostly between 3,000 and 7,000 feet. Higher and lower elevations receive progressively less moisture. The wettest months are between October and April.

The islands were formed by shield volcanoes rising slowly from the ocean floor to form gently sloping, symmetrical mountains. Today's rugged peaks and valleys were shaped by millennia of erosion that faithfully reflect the invariable weather patterns.

Erosion is increasingly evident proceeding northwest from the gentle slopes of the young island of Hawaii to the ancient and precipitous Na Pali Coast of Kauai. Generally, the deepest valleys begin where rainfall is heaviest, on the north or northeast sides of each island. The highest sea cliffs and most rugged coastlines are usually on the north coasts, where wave action is strongest.

Clothing and Equipment

A pleasant part of hiking in Hawaii is that relatively little equipment is needed. However, this is *not* true of the hikes on Haleakala and Mauna Loa which require equipment comparable to that used for mountain climbing on the mainland, such as, tents, heavy wool clothing, and rain gear. The temperature drops 3 to 5 degrees Fahrenheit for every 1,000 feet gained in elevation. Hikes into the wet areas above 2,000 feet can be unpleasant and dangerous, if the traveler becomes wet or is overtaken by darkness. Waterproof and wool clothing should be carried, the latter because it retains some warmth even when wet. Exposure has been a complication in many rescues.

Stout, broken-in boots are needed for hikes on the high mountains or over rough lava; tennis shoes are fine for short hikes. Long pants are the rule because of heavy brush along the trails. Sunglasses are desirable near the sea and goggles are mandatory in the high, snow-covered mountains. Many visitors from the mainland can receive painful sunburns and therefore should use protective lotion. Rain gear near sea level is optional; some prefer to hike in light clothing, get wet in the warm rain, and dry out later. After all, one can only get so wet. Tents may be required for camping in some areas. They are necessary at high elevations, and may be of value in keeping out insects and rain. Plastic ground covers can double as ponchos and picnic cloths. Insect repellent, flashlights, and a compass are useful. Usually only light sleeping bags are needed. Unfortunately, frame packs may not be allowed on buses.

Plants and Animals

The isolation of the Hawaiian Islands allowed the evolution of life forms fascinatingly different from those found in continental regions. In prehistoric times, plants and animals traveled great distances from their original homes to flourish in the islands, free from their natural enemies. In time, these original species evolved into new life forms found nowhere else, filling the various ecological niches in these islands.

The pigs, dogs, rats, and fire brought by the original Polynesians began the process of ecological damage. The original plants and animals suffered even more grievously when they came into contact with the rest of the world. These gentle life forms, no longer protected by thorns, poisons, deep roots, vigorous regenerative powers, and resistance to disease, could not compete successfully against the hardy, newly imported life forms. Foreign diseases, carelessly introduced species of plants and insects, voracious livestock, and wild fire have destroyed vast portions of the original flora, and have led to the extermination of whole species of desirable plants and ani-

mals. No other state's life forms have seen and continue to see such a thorough destruction. Domestic and wild livestock were steadily destroying the forested areas on all the islands until the early part of this century. When the water supplies became imperiled, the government set aside forest areas for protection, and the wild livestock was destroyed. Sugar plantation interests and government agencies began the reforestation of previously wasted areas with native and imported species of trees. Norfolk Island pine, ironwood, eucalyptus, and even redwood are some of the introduced tree species used in reforestation.

Many of the trails described in this book lead through such plantings, now grown into large forests. Other trails located in the most inaccessible and unfrequented regions of the Hawaiian Islands lead higher to forests largely untouched by this devastation. Sadly, even there, extinction gains ground.

Dangers, Pests, and Precautions

The wet regions of the Hawaiian Islands are mostly covered by impenetrable vegetation, and the topograghy of many portions of the islands can be exceptionally rough. Know where you came from at all times. If a trail dwindles away, it is probably a false one, such as a dead-ending hunters' route. Retrace your steps to see if you have missed the correct trail. Above all, STAY ON THE TRAIL. The rock is universally rotten and portable handholds abound; cliffs and thick vegetation make cross-country travel unwise. Off the trail, hunters may mistake you for an animal. Vegetation may crowd in and hide drop-offs. If totally lost or stranded, it is usually safest to wait for day and attract help. If you attempt to find your own way out, it is usually better to follow ridges, since the going and visibility there may be better than in gulches. Rain, even far upstream, may make streams impassable or cause flash floods. Beware of falling rocks in waterfalls. Hikers following the sea coast should not be lulled into thinking that all waves are the same size. "Rogue" waves, far larger than usual, occasionally sweep the unwary into the sea. Tidal waves sweep the beaches at rare intervals. If you experience an earthquake near the sea, run uphill immediately.

Mosquitoes are comparative newcomers to the Hawaiian Islands. The first species were introduced in the early 1800's, reputedly by whalers who emptied contaminated water casks brought ashore for refilling. Relatively few species of mosquitoes are present, and not all ecological niches are filled; thus, few are encountered above 2,800 feet, and all species tend to avoid strong sunlight. In low areas, breezy dry spots are best for camping. The local mosquitoes are not as suicidally ferocious as those found in more northerly latitudes. In time, however, even these rapacious pests may be carelessly introduced. Mosquitoes have been the factor most limiting to the survival of native forest birds. Due to avian malaria spread by mosquitoes, most native forest birds are surviving only above the elevations where mosquitoes thrive. Black widow spiders are found in Hawaii, as in all states. Poisonous centipedes and scorpions are occasionally found near sea level and can inflict stings about as painful as bee stings. No dangerous land snakes are present. Pigs may attack, if disturbed. Sharks in the waters off the beaches are not noted for being man-eaters; however, some have broken this general rule. Waves and currents are a more real danger.

Water, food, compass, current maps, and the usual emergency and first aid gear should be carried. A flashlight is especially important on late afternoon hikes. Because of the low latitude, night descends with unexpected rapidity. Allow ample time to arrive before nightfall.

Even flowing water may be contaminated by upstream animals and human beings. It is safest to treat it. Poison oak and poison ivy are not found on the Hawaiian Islands; however, some persons are allergic to the mango tree and its fruit. The bark of the paper bark tree is highly irritating when wet and should not be used for toilet paper. Numerous plants can be poisonous, if eaten, used for cooking skewers, or rubbed into skin.

Crime and violence have increased in Hawaii, just as in the rest of the United States. Hikers and especially campers are not immune. Theft is a major problem, particularly in areas frequented by tourists. Valuables should not be left unattended or left locked in cars. Vehicles left unattended are sometimes broken into or damaged. Marijuana patches must be strictly avoided since they may be jealously and dangerously guarded. The patches are usually carefully hidden and are less likely to be found along well-traveled trails. This is yet another reason to stay on the known trails.

Hiking on the more hazardous trails and camping should be in groups of three or more. Leave your plans with a responsible person. Respect private property and stay out of *kapu* (closed) watersheds or military areas. Pack out whatever you bring in. Clean your shoes and clothes to avoid spreading seeds.

Fires

In the warm lowland climate campfires add little comfort. Firewood is scarce at higher, cooler elevations and fires outside of designated firepits are wisely prohibited in the national parks and most other areas. If cooking cannot be dispensed with, a gas stove should be used. Purchase stove fuel locally, since airlines forbid its presence on planes. Fire danger is great and caution with fires cannot be stressed enough. Rain forest conditions give a false sense of security. Sunny skies and steady winds can dry up a rain-soaked morning forest and, through someone's carelessness, turn it into a blazing inferno by midafternoon. Heavy underbrush, steep slopes, high winds, and peat soils make fires extremely difficult to control. Dry humus and accumulated material on the ground is often so deep that a fire can start, burn through a wet top layer, and progress underground to burst out later and devastate large areas.

Transportation

Reduced fares may be available for inter-island jet flights in connection with flights from the mainland, if booked simultaneously. It is unnecessary to reverse tracks to see the island chain, since there are direct flights between the mainland and several islands. Reduced fares may also be available for off-hour flights, standbys, and military personnel. The small planes used by some airlines fly at low elevations, thus allowing good visibility. Flights by the north coast of Molokai and the north coast of Hawaii are particularly scenic.

Bus transportation is extensive on Oahu, limited on Hawaii, and, at present, very limited or unavailable elsewhere. Hitchhiking, though possibly illegal, is fairly common. Rental cars are available on all the islands with rates varying widely. Rental agencies occasionally refuse to rent to campers and hikers.

Camping

Campgrounds are found throughout the state and are adminstered by the National Park Service, the State of Hawaii, the counties, or private organizations. Camping areas that are close to the trails have been mentioned, but there are many more. Some campgrounds, especially those close to roads, have a poor reputation for public safety. Reservations and permits are always required in advance from the offices of the agencies for the use of cabins and camping areas. These agencies will send detailed and current information about permits, camping, cabins, and hiking. Make reservations and acquire permits early. The statistical summaries in the trail descriptions include the names of the administering agencies.

Addresses for Permits and Current Information

Access permits are required for a few of the trails. Some require trailhead registration. This information is noted in the trail description. Conditions change rapidly; therefore, obtain current information from the appropriate agency for each of the islands.

Island of Hawaii

Hawaii Volcanoes National Park
P.O. Box 52
Hawaii, HI 96718-0052
(808)985-6000

Pu'uhonua-o-Honaunau
National Historical Park
Honaunau, Kona, HI 96726
(808)328-2326

Hiking on the Kalalau Trail

Division of Forestry and Wildlife
P.O. Box 4849, 19 East Kawili Street
Hilo, HI 96720
(808)974-4221

Division of State Parks
P.O. Box 936, 75 Aupuni Street
Hilo, HI 96721-0936
(808)974-6200

County of Hawaii
Department of Parks and Recreation
25 Aupuni Street
Hilo, HI 96720
(808)961-8311

Island of Maui

Haleakala National Park
P.O. Box 369
Makawao, Maui, HI 96768
(808)572-4400

Division of Forestry and Wildlife
54 So. High Street
Wailuku, Maui, HI 96793
(808)984-8100

Division of State Parks
54 So. High Street
Wailuku, Maui, HI 96793
(808)984-8109

Maui County Parks Department
1580 Kaahumanu Avenue
Wailuku, Maui, HI 96793
(808)243-7389

Island of Lanai

Lanai Company, Inc.
P.O. Box 310
Island of Lanai, HI 96763
(800)321-4666; (808)565-3800

Island of Molokai

Division of Forestry and Wildlife
54 So. High Street
Wailuku, Maui, HI 96793
(808)984-8100

Division of State Parks
54 So. High Street
Wailuku, Maui, HI 96793
(808)984-8109

County of Maui
Department of Parks and Recreation
Kaunakakai, Molokai, HI 96748
(808)553-3221

The Nature Conservancy of Hawaii
P.O. Box 220
Kualapuu, Molokai, HI 96757
(808)553-5236

Island of Oahu

Division of Forestry and Wildlife
P.O. Box 621
1151 Punchbowl Street
Honolulu, HI 96813
(808)587-0166

Division of State Parks
P.O. Box 621
1151 Punchbowl Street
Honolulu, HI 96809
(808)587-0300

City and County of Honolulu
Department of Parks and Recreation
650 South King Street
Honolulu, HI 96813
(808)523-4525 or (808)523-4527

Ho'omaluhia Botanical Garden
45-680 Luluku Road
Kaneohe, HI 96744
(808)233-7323

The Nature Conservancy of Hawaii
1116 Smith Street, Suite 201
Honolulu, HI 96817
(808)537-4508

Island of Kauai

Division of Forestry and Wildlife
3060 Eiwa Street, Rm. 306
Lihue, Kauai, HI 96766-1875
(808)274-3433

Division of State Parks
3060 Eiwa Street, Rm. 306
Lihue, Kauai, HI 96766
(808)274-3444

County of Kauai
Division of Parks and Recreation
4444 Rice Street, Suite 150
Lihue, Kauai 96766
(808)241-6660

Kokee Lodge, Manager
P.O. Box 819
Waimea, Kauai, HI 96796
(808)335-6061

Maps

United States Geological Survey
Federal Center
P.O. Box 25286
Denver, CO 80225
(888)ASK-USGS
(888)275-8747

Bus Information

"The Bus"
(808)848-5555

Iao Needle

Island of Hawaii

Ancient Hawaiian legend relates that Pele, the Polynesian goddess of volcanoes, made her early home in Kauai. Dissatisfied, she moved south along the chain of islands, eventually residing in the southeastern portion of the Island of Hawaii. Interestingly, this path follows geologic history. The Hawaiian island chain was formed by volcanism from northwest to southeast. Some geologists argue that the volcanoes erupted along a fault line. Others contend that one island after another was formed as the earth's crust gradually moved northwest over a stationary hot spot far beneath the earth's surface. In any event, this volcanism created the Island of Hawaii and in the process provided unmatched hiking experiences.

The 4,038-square-mile Island of Hawaii has 63 percent of all the land area of the Hawaiian Islands. The trails are generally longer than those on the other islands, and the scale of the land forms is far larger. However, since Hawaii is the newest of the islands, it has not yet experienced the full effects of erosion. Large, lava-covered areas, especially in the west, are quite barren. They may be dry because of the rain shadows of the island's volcanic mountains or because the mountains are too far above the rain clouds borne by the trade winds. Furthermore, the lava is still so new that deep soil has not had a chance to form and water quickly disappears below the surface. The unique native forests that once did retain water and covered many areas have been largely destroyed by grazing animals.

The Island of Hawaii was formed by five great volcanoes: Mauna Loa, Mauna Kea, Hualalei, Kilauea, and Kohala. Of these

Fresh lava — first plants

only the oldest, Kohala, has eroded as much as the volcanoes on the older islands such as Kauai and Oahu. The most spectacular valleys and waterfalls are in the Kohala Mountains. The lower north and east slopes of Mauna Kea are somewhat less eroded, but still offer pleasant waterfalls and pools. The Akaka Falls Trail leads to one of the most scenic of these waterfalls.

Active examples of the geologic processes that formed all of the Hawaiian Islands are found in Hawaii Volcanoes National Park. Park trails lead past volcanic vents, over still-cooling lava, and to the top of world's largest shield volcano. The Kilauea Iki Trail leads into one of the most volcanically active parts of the world. It is so active that

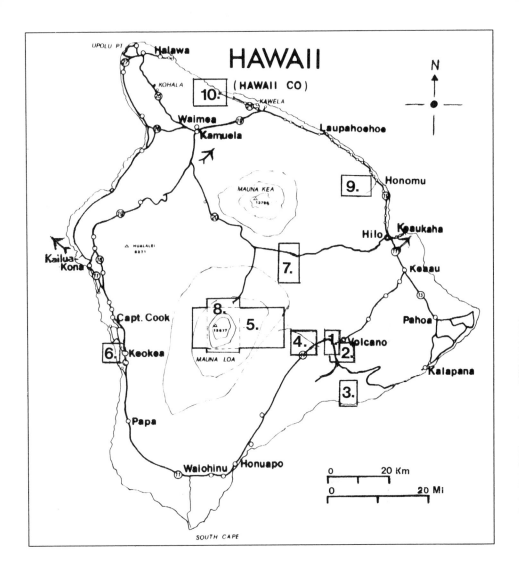

HAWAII
(HAWAII CO)

volcanism will perhaps soon destroy the trail itself. The trails up Mauna Loa are more like mountain climbs than hikes, since they lead into high, frigid regions devoid of plant and animal life. Careful preparation is required because the cold can be extreme and because of the danger of serious sunburn. The great elevation and distances of these trails make them exhausting, but also unforgettable.

Two trails, Puu Oo and Kipuka Puaulu (Bird Park), lead through another type of volcanic phenomenon, the *kipuka*, which is an area undamaged by flows of lava. Protected by the rough surrounding lava from some of the worst depredations of livestock,

kipukas provide good opportunities to observe rare native Hawaiian plants and birds.

The route, Halape via Keauhou Trail, in Hawaii Volcanoes National Park leads steeply down extensive lava flows to Halape's white-sand beach, formed after the earthquake and tidal wave of 1975. Among the breakers lies the site of the idyllic grove of coconut trees that once graced Halape.

Camping is excellent and safest in Hawaii Volcanoes National Park. The park headquarters at Kilauea Visitor Center provides current information on the well-cared-for campgrounds, cabins, and wilderness campsites.

The Waipio-Waimanu Trail leads along

Halape after the earthquake

the base of the rugged Kohala Mountains into an area as isolated as any in the Hawaiian Islands. There, large valleys which once teemed with people and were centers of civilization are now almost empty. The trail passes by the ruins of ancient Hawaiian villages and through abandoned groves of fruit trees. It ends at long, beautiful, black-sand Waimanu Beach.

Kipuka forest — Puu Oo Trail

Thurston Lava Tube

1. Iliahi Loop
1¹/₂ hours, loop trip
175 calories; easier
1.3 miles, loop trip
Highest point: 3980 feet
Lowest point: 3750 feet
Hawaii Volcanoes National Park

The "Iliahi Loop" Trail is made up of the Sandalwood Trail and portions of the Crater Rim and Halemaumau Trails. This popular, short hike starts from the Kilauea Visitor Center (Hawaii Volcanoes National Park Headquarters). Along its route the trail passes through ohia forest with large amaumau tree ferns, then climbs along a cliff overlooking Kilauea Crater. As the trail nears the crater rim it comes to cracks issuing hot vapor from water flowing onto the hot rocks beneath the surface.

The cliff edge portion of the trail overlooking the treetops is particularly good for seeing the small native birds which inhabit the canopy of ohia forests. The most common bird is the apapane, a five-inch-long, bright-red bird with black wings and tail. Also fairly common is the iiwi, which is similar, but has a curved beak. Both are most active in early morning or evening.

ROUTE: From Kilauea Visitor Center circle around the edge of the parking lot counterclockwise then go just across Crater Rim Drive to the access to the Crater Rim Trail, which is marked by logos of a hiker. Follow this trail for 75 yards, paralleling Crater Rim Drive. The trail comes to an intersection with a sign showing trail mileages and directions. Keep right and follow the sign which reads "Sandalwood Trail 0.3 miles." The trail soon descends steps and comes to another intersection, which is the start of the loop portion of the trip. The signs give mileages to both ends of the Sandalwood Trail.

Start the loop by taking the trail to the left, the Halemaumau Trail. It descends through a deep native forest of ohia trees, hapuu (tree ferns) and amaumau ferns.

Steam vents

Markers along the way identify native plants. Native birds call and cheery crickets chirp as they rub their wings to attract mates. These crickets evolved here over millions of years into a unique species with unique songs.

After 0.2 miles from the start, the Halemaumau Trail reaches a turnoff, right, onto the Sandalwood Trail. Follow the Sandalwood Trail, which threads its way along a cliff edge and gradually climbs uphill to the Crater Rim Trail. Along this portion of the route there are fine views of Puu Puia cinder cone, Kilauea Crater and Halemaumau.

Fern and Ohia forest

As the trail reaches the crater rim it passes by steaming vents, surrounded by luxuriant growths of little ferns and mosses enjoying perpetual summer. Shortly after reaching the crater rim, the Sandalwood Trail comes to an intersection of trails, with the Crater Rim Trail running left and right, and the Sulfur Banks Trail straight ahead. Turn to the right onto the Crater Rim Trail and follow it 0.3 miles to complete the loop. Then continue back up the steps on the Crater Rim Trail to the Kilauea Visitor Center.

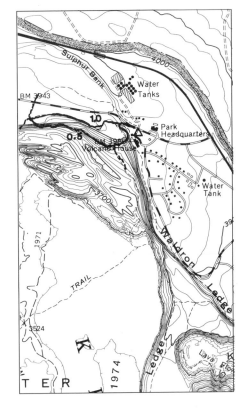

2. Kilauea Iki

2¹/₂ hours, loop trip
500 calories; easier
3 miles, loop trip
Highest point: 3900 feet
Lowest point: 3500 feet
Hawaii Volcanoes National Park

Kilauea Iki means "little Kilauea." It is almost a scale model of large Kilauea Crater, located just to the west. Although smaller, it has provided spectacular volcanic shows. The Kilauea Iki Trail has been selected from several interesting trails across the floors and along the rims of both craters because it offers in a short distance varied and impressive evidence of Hawaii's volcanism.

Kilauea Iki is world famous for the great eruption of 1959 in which a lava fountain at one point reached 1900 feet high. Spewing from the southwest side of Kilauea Iki, it half filled the crater and put on a spectacular display for 36 days. Films of this eruption are shown hourly at park headquarters.

ROUTE: Drive 29 miles southwest of Hilo on Highway 11 to Hawaii Volcanoes National Park. Turn off left to the park headquarters one mile after passing the park entrance. From the park headquarters proceed on Crater Rim Road south (left) approximately 1.5 miles to the Kilauea Iki overlook on the west (right) side of the road. Parking is available at the overlook, and the trailhead is clearly marked on the north end of the parking lot. Walk counterclockwise along the north rim of Kilauea Iki Crater, passing junctions with other trails in the area. About 0.7 miles from the trailhead, the trail descends through a handsome forest of tree ferns. One mile from the trailhead, it joins a connector to the Byron Ledge Trail. A short side trip on the Byron Ledge Trail offers an impressive view of Kilauea Crater. From the junction with the Byron Ledge Trail, the Kilauea Iki Trail starts side-hilling down the wall of Kilauea Iki Crater onto its floor and past the vent of the 1959 lava fountain. Many ohelo bushes, loaded with succulent red berries in the summer, may be found along the way. These berries are one of the earliest plants to appear after volcanic activity has scorched the ground. Tradition has it that you must offer some of the berries to Pele, the goddess of volcanism, before eating any or you will incur her wrath. Since at this point you are about to walk across almost a mile of still-cooling lava, past a dormant volcanic vent, you might consider this tradition carefully.

Past the vent, the trail leads across the crater's flat floor on lava which sends up clouds of steam where water reaches the still-hot rocks beneath the surface. Note how ferns and small mosses are slowly pioneering this area. Proceed directly across the crater to its east side where a stone cairn marks the trail up the east wall. The trail switchbacks through a forest of giant tree ferns and ends at Crater Rim Road and a junction with the Crater Rim Trail. Immediately across the road a 0.3-mile loop trail leads to and through Thurston Lava Tube, a worthwhile side trip. Return to your starting point by following the Crater Rim Trail along the rim of Kilauea Iki for 0.3 miles.

Kilauea Iki Crater

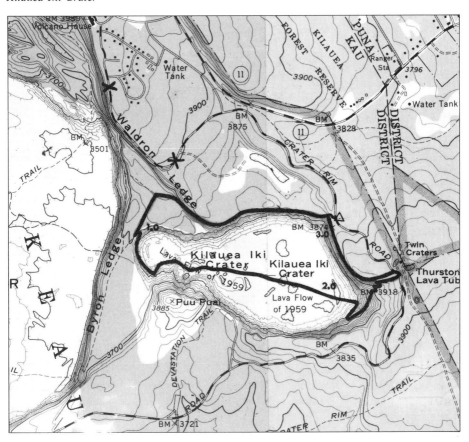

3. Halape via Keauhou Trail

2 days, round trip
4 hours down; 6 hours up
3000 calories; hardest
16.1 miles, round trip with loop
Highest point: 2680 feet
Lowest point: sea level
Hawaii Volcanoes National Park

The wilderness campsite at the coastal oasis of Halape, on the hot, dry, south Kau Coast is reached by long, barren trails. Halape's green cove and small, white coral beach are rarities on this desolate coast. Among the breakers lies the site of the idyllic grove of coconut trees that once graced Halape. The earthquake of 1975, accompanied by huge, deadly tsunami, submerged much of Halape. A replanted grove of coconut trees taps the underground fresh water which floats on the ocean water underlying the coast.

The south Kau Coast becomes overburdened with layers of lava, which periodically causes it to drop and move outward, resulting in sudden and huge tsunami, as in 1868 and in 1975. In the scale of geologic time, such earthquakes occur often, as evidenced by fault lines visible along the coast. If you feel a large earthquake while at the coast, stand not upon the order of your going, but run uphill at once.

Register at Kilauea Visitor Center for wilderness camping and obtain the latest brochures for the coastal area. Carry a ground pad and an insect proof, free-standing tent. Wear boots with good ankle support, and take clothing which gives some shade. Be prepared for a hard, hot uphill return. Do not attempt this in the afternoon heat: the greatest danger on this trail is exposure to the sun. People have died on this trail of failing to drink water. Bring plenty, and be sure to drink it. Eat snacks. Do not be overtaken by night, which falls rapidly at this latitude. Leave early.

ROUTE: From Kilauea Visitor Center drive south on Crater Rim Drive for 3 miles around Kilauea Iki Crater to Chain of Craters Road. Follow Chain of Craters Road south about 6 miles to the pullout at Mau Loa o Mauna Ulu. The Keauhou Trail begins here, gradually descending for two miles, first over recent pahoehoe lava, and then through sparse ohia forest and grassland. It reaches grass covered country and a steeper descent at the top of Poliokeawe Pali. The trail descends the pali and at 4.8 miles it reaches a spur trail, Puueo Pali, to the right. Instead of continuing down directly to Keauhou Landing, take the spur trail across the slope for 1.3 miles to reach the Hilina Pali Trail. Go left and follow the trail down for 1.6 miles to Halape.

At the beach, avoid stepping on sea urchins when wading. Also be careful not to interfere with the rare nesting hawkspill turtles and resting green sea turtles. Lights or fires confuse them and food left out attracts predators.

The shelter at Halape has been prudently situated well inland to protect it from the tsunami. The campsites are east of the beach and cove. There is brackish water in a large crack 75 yards directly inland. Use care to keep it free of soap and sun screen. Water may be available from the tank at the shelter (treat it). Use a tent to avoid ants and the unpleasantness of night roaming cockroaches, centipedes, and scorpions.

To make the loop trip via Keauhou Landing, parallel the coast east along the Puna Coast Trail for 1.6 miles. At Keauhou, there is also a shelter and a camping area. To return, take the Keauhou Trail, which leads directly uphill from the shelter. At 2.0 miles the trail meets the turnoff taken earlier. Continue up to return to Mau Loa o Mauna Ulu trailhead as you came.

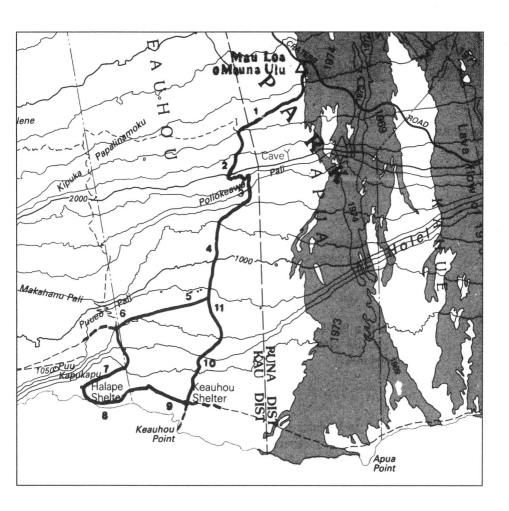

Looking back at Halape on the way to Keauhou Landing

4. Kipuka Puaulu (Bird Park)

1 hour, loop trip
200 calories; easiest
1.2 miles, loop trip
Highest point: 4180 feet
Lowest point: 3940 feet
Hawaii Volcanoes National Park

This trail provides an easy opportunity to view a *kipuka* (an area missed by surrounding lava flows) and a largely unspoiled native Hawaiian forest. This kipuka, like kipukas at higher, less verdant elevations along the Puu Oo Trail (described later), provides numerous examples of native Hawaiian plants and related animals. The National Park Service has done a commendable job of maintaining the trail and labeling the plants for visitors. A booklet written by the Hawaii Natural History Association describing the labeled plants on this self-guided trail is available at the park headquarters.

ROUTE: To reach the trail from Hilo drive 31 miles southwest on Highway 11 to Mauna Loa Road, located about 2.3 miles past the Hawaii Volcanoes National Park headquarters turnoff. Follow Mauna Loa Road 1.6 miles to the parking area next to the trailhead. The trailhead is well marked with a display of some of the more common plants and birds you will see during this pleasant, easy hike. The grade is gradual, the route is obvious and the path is well maintained.

Near the display, the trail passes through a fence designed to keep out wild pigs. Close this gate since it is protection for this fragile area from these animals. Just beyond the gate the path joins the loop. Take the left-hand fork around the loop's gentle course. After 0.5 miles, a short side trail leads left (north) to a large koa tree, about 50 yards off the trail. From this turn-off the rest of the loop returns generally downhill to the starting point. Numerous native Hawaiian birds may be seen in the nearby treetops during the hike. The most common

Giant ohia tree

is the apapane, a little, bright-red bird with black wings and tail. It is especially fond of the nectar of the red-blossomed ohia lehua trees. The iiwi bird, also fairly common, is colored like the apapane, but is somewhat larger and has a curved bill. These birds and others are best seen early in the morning or at evening, especially after a rain.

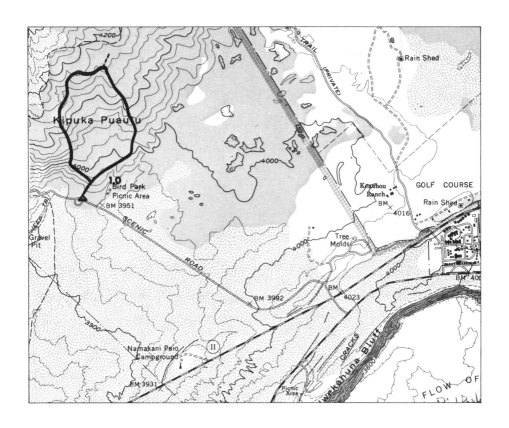

Kipuka Puaulu Trail

5. Mauna Loa via Red Hill

3-4 days; 18 hours up, 12 hours down
8700 calories; hardest
36.6 miles, round trip
Highest point: 13,250 feet
Lowest point: 6662 feet
Hawaii Volcanoes National Park

In terms of physical effort, the climb up the Mauna Loa Trail via Red Hill to Mauna Loa Cabin is one of the hardest hikes in the Hawaiian Islands. It is also perhaps the most memorable. Mauna Loa's volume is enormous — on the order of 10,000 cubic miles. Mt. Shasta, by comparison, has a volume of only 80 cubic miles. Mauna Loa (long mountain) and Mauna Kea (white mountain) are the highest mountains in the world — if one takes the elevation starting from their bases on the ocean floor. From the ocean floor, the mountains rise approximately 30,000 feet to their summits, making each formation taller than Mt. Everest. Even with a head start at 6,662 feet above sea level, it is truly a long, long way to the top of Mauna Loa.

It is said of Mount Fuji, "He who does not climb Fuji once is a fool; he who climbs it twice is also a fool." Some would say the same of Mauna Loa. The written word, however, cannot express the experience of hiking along the great northeast rift of Mauna Loa, past mile upon mile of iridescent ash. Nor can words express the experience of rising before dawn and watching the faintly increasing morning light creep across huge Mokuaweoweo Caldera, a great lake of still steaming lava which melts every few years to run down the mountain and build further the Island of Hawaii. Not a living thing is in view. The air is cold and rare.

ROUTE: Drive southwest on Highway 11 from Hilo to the Hawaii Volcanoes National Park headquarters. You must register with the rangers there for the climb and for use of both Red Hill Cabin, halfway along the trail, and Mauna Loa Cabin, located on

South across Mokuaweoweo Caldera

the east side of Mokuaweoweo Caldera. These cabins are equipped with mattresses and bunks. You need halazone tablets for purifying the water which may have been collected from the cabin roofs. Check with the rangers for current information and regarding the suitability of your equipment, including heavy wool clothing and sleeping bag (in plastic sacks), rain gear, goggles for snow, water, food, flashlight, sunburn protection, and other mountaineering equipment.

Arctic conditions with considerable snow, extreme cold, fog, and high winds and rain can occur at any time of year on Mauna Loa. The weather may be cloudy for days at a time and the trail obscured by snow. Molten lava and noxious fumes may spew out unexpectedly from volcanic vents underlying the mountain. The rough *aa* lava off the trail is torturesome going. Take into account the effect of elevation along the upper portions of this trail. Nearly everyone living close to sea level is affected by exertion at these altitudes near 13,000 feet. Consider the miles at these altitudes to be twice as long as those at sea level. Headaches, pounding heart, and rapid breathing are indications of the effects of altitude; the only immediate remedy is rest and more oxygen. The rough lava along this trail will quickly destroy all but heavy boots.

From the park headquarters, drive on Highway 11 west, about 2.3 miles to the start of Mauna Loa Road and follow it to the end. Mauna Loa Road climbs for 11 miles to end near the 6,662 foot level at a waterless lookout and parking area. The trailhead is located just uphill from the lookout. The trail at first contours east across the slope for a short distance, then passes uphill through a gate. Close this gate to prevent damage to the park by wild goats. After the gate the trail leads up through steadily diminishing vegetation to Red Hill Cabin 7.0 miles (4-6 hours) from the trailhead. For its entire extent the trail is easy to follow unless covered by snow or obscured by poor visibility. It is marked by the passage of others and *ahu* (stone cairns) located at intervals.

From Red Hill Cabin, which is the first night's resting place, the trail leads up through land almost devoid of vegetation and covered with lava flows of bizarre shapes and colors, past splatter cones and across large volcanic faults to Mauna Loa Cabin approximately 11.3 miles (12 hours) away. The trail from Red Hill is in the path of the 1984 flows. Follow the most recent ahu markers to find the most accurate route. There is no water readily available along this trail and the lower portions can

Mauna Loa Trail going over pahoehoe lava

be hot and dry. At 16.3 miles from the start, the trail reaches North Pit, the northern "bay" of the great Mokuaweoweo Caldera. There, four trails intersect. The Summit Trail leads to the right along the caldera's west rim to the summit. The Observatory Trail leads to the right (north), down to the Observatory. The Cabin Trail (considered here as part of the Mauna Loa Trail) leads south across North Pit to Mauna Loa Cabin on the east side of the caldera.

In former years this cabin was reached by another trail, now abandoned, which followed the caldera's east rim. The older trail is now poorly marked and is by no means as interesting as the route across the floor of North Pit. The trail to the cabin across North Pit drops a short distance to the pit floor and then leads straight south across the smooth, flat lava. After crossing the pit floor, the trail leads up and generally south to Mokuaweoweo Caldera's rim, skirting the southwest rim of Lua Poholo, a deep secondary caldera. The trail then continues along the caldera's rim to the cabin. About 0.3 miles due south of the cabin, ice and

snow may often be found in a crevice marked by ahu.

If caught by darkness on a clear summer night, follow the trail across the caldera by setting a course on the Southern Cross, visible close to the horizon. Do not stumble into Lua Poholo in the dark. Approach its rim and all other such formations with caution.

Stay the second night at the cabin. From it you may wish to take the climb to Mauna Loa's summit, retracing your steps to the junction of the Mauna Loa Summit Trail with the trail to the cabin. From the junction follow the signed trail, marked with ahu, along the west rim of the caldera to the summit. The nine-mile round trip at these altitudes should be considered an all-day affair, though route-finding is no problem. As an alternative, explore the southwest portion of the caldera near South Pit, which has lava flows and fields of golden pumice from volcanism in the 1940's.

Be sure to inform the park headquarters of your return. Failure to do so is unforgivable.

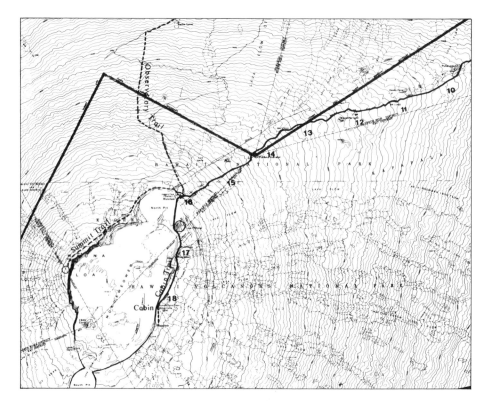

Red Hill Cabin

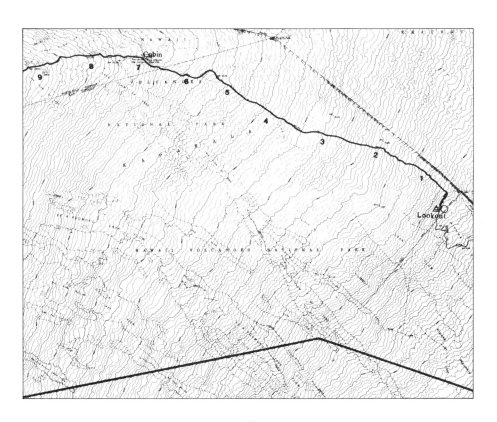

6. Pu'uhonua-o-Honaunau

1 hour, loop trip
300 calories, easiest
1.6 miles, loop trip
Highest point: 40 feet
Lowest point: sea level
Pu'uhonua-o-Honaunau National
    Historical Park

Ramp over Keanae'e Cliff

Pu'uhonua-o-Honaunau National Park preserves the ancient ruins of several heiau, fish ponds, house foundations, sled ramps, trails from different periods of Hawaiian history, and a great stone wall, within whose boundaries *kapu* breakers and the vanquished could find refuge. From the visitor center a short interpretive trail meanders by re-created models of ancient houses, fearsome wooden carvings, and the impressive stonework.

Beyond the interpretive area, lie the routes of an early foot path and a nineteenth century horse trail leading south to a stone ramp over Keanae'e Cliff. In the early days Keanae'e Cliff, with its "frozen waterfall" of lava, was an obstacle to travelers along this coast. It was passable only at a low point where the cliff meets Alahaka Bay. The prehistoric foot trail of the type marked by a single row of smooth stones reached the cliff at this low point after hugging the coast to avoid dreaded *kapu* areas. With the introduction of horses and the end of the *kapu* system, a new, more direct, inland horse trail, was built, marked by "kerbstones" on either side. South of Keanae'e's housesites the new trail basically followed the ancient foot trail. This was probably the route mentioned in Mark Twain's letters about the area. The substantial ramp now climbing the cliff was built around 1868. For more information about the old trails, see *Trails* by Russell A. Apple, Bishop Museum Press.

ROUTE: This seaside park is on the Kona (leeward, west) coast at the bottom of the road descending 1000 feet in three miles from the turnoff at the Keokea intersection on Highway 11. The loop through the inter-

pretive area begins at the visitor center and is described in materials provided by the park.

To reach the points of interest farther south, proceed along the road from the visitor center to the seaside picnic area and then about a third of a mile south along the shore until shortly before the shoreline is indented by Alahaka Bay. There, about 100 paces inland, past various stonework, is the straight, level 1871 horse trail. Proceed south from this junction to climb the ramp. The trail then eventually passes out of the park area. A narrow, perhaps dangerous, lava tube starts immediately on the left side of the ramp and leads under it to the sea.

The 1871 trail leading straight north from the ramp provides a good return route, passing by prospering introduced dryland plants which, being unpalatable, stickery, or poisonous, have defied the appetites of goats and cattle. It soon crosses the course of a rock sled ramp seen lying uphill on the right. When covered with pili grass and mud in ancient times the ramp must have been the scene of many a merry slide. In an act eloquently bespeaking the new age, the royal sled ramp was partially demolished to provide fill rock for the horse trail.

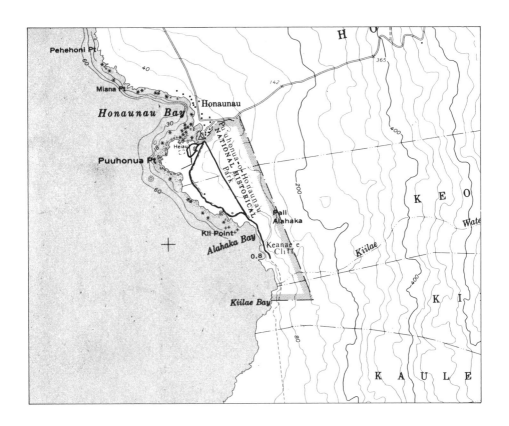

Kapu

7. Puu Oo

4 hours, round trip
1100 calories, harder
7.4 miles, round trip
Highest point: 5800 feet
Lowest point: 5750 feet
Division of Forestry and Wildlife

Hawaii is a young volcanic island, growing at a high rate by the standards of geologic time. Lava flows have frequently covered large areas of the island even in recent years. One such area, located in the Ainahou and Upper Waiakea Forest Reserves, is traversed by the Puu Oo Trail, which provides excellent examples of the return of vegetation to areas covered by lava flows.

The most recent volcanic activity seems to be limited to areas farther south, in Hawaii Volcanoes National Park, but the flows crossed by the Puu Oo Trail are by no means ancient.

Early cattle ranchers had to use the trail to drive their herds over the rough, scoriaceous lava beds of *aa* (rough) lava that separated the saddle lands between Mauna Kea and Mauna Loa, where their cattle grazed, from the market at the seaport of Hilo. Although Hilo is not far from this region, as the crow flies, the only practical way through the *aa* lava led down the Puu Oo Trail to the town of Volcano near Hawaii Volcanoes National Park. From there the cattle could be driven on down the road to Hilo or, in still earlier times, to the ocean to the south. The trail has not been used for this purpose for many years. Yet, it may still be followed by looking closely for the *ahu* (stone cairns) and other trail markers.

The trail crosses the lava flows of 1855, 1881, and 1935, among others, which provide good examples of both *aa* and *pahoehoe* (smooth) lava. Different types and thicknesses of vegetation grow on each of these flows depending on the age of the flow and the type of lava. The trail also

Pahoehoe lava

crosses large *kipukas* where the lava flows have by-passed the old growth of ohia, pukeawe, ohelo, and majestic koa trees, populated with a wide assortment of endemic bird species. Native ferns, lichens, and mosses are found along the way. Rainfall in the area is up to 80 inches a year, but the land appears quite dry because of the good drainage of the underlying lava. Since few people take this trail, and ohelo berries are abundant, bird watching is well rewarded, especially early in the morning and toward evening. Native birds, such as the apapane, iiwi, and amakihi abound. There is even a chance of seeing the rare nene goose.

ROUTE: Take the Saddle Road (Hwy 200) west from Hilo until about 0.4 miles after the 22 mile marker, near the boundary of the Ainahou and the Upper Waiakea Forest Reserves. The trail begins on the left (south) side of the highway. A wooden sign marks the trailhead. Parking is available.

Follow the trail from the parking area south along a course roughly parallel to and west of a powerline and service road which

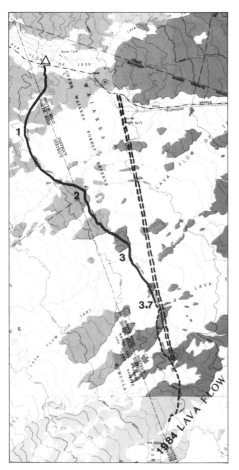

Amaumau fern (sadleria)

are visible in the distance. The trail is difficult to follow at points. Look for *ahu* and other signs of the trail, being quick to retrace your steps if lost. After about 3.7 miles the trail joins the powerline road. This is a good turnaround point since you have already passed the most interesting portion of the trail. Further on, the trail has been obliterated by the 1984 lava flows and permission may be required for access. From the turnaround point you have the option of returning via the powerline road and the Saddle Road. Since the trail is located at nearly 6000 feet, it can be cool and you should dress warmly. There is neither potable water nor a campground on the trail.

8. Mauna Loa via the Observatory

2 days; 10 hours up, 6 hours down
3500 calories; hardest
12 miles, round trip
Highest point: 13,250 feet
Lowest point: 11,060 feet
Hawaii Volcanoes National Park

A road from the north leading to the 11,000-foot level provides access to the lesser used of the two routes for climbing to Mauna Loa Cabin on the east rim of the Mokuaweoweo Caldera. The trail does not follow a rift zone and, therefore, is not as interesting geologically as the Mauna Loa Trail (via Red Hill), which is the recommended route. It does, however, offer good views of Mauna Kea. The climb is long. It is best to start walking at first light and in any event not later than early morning.

Morning climb

ROUTE: Register for the climb and the cabin with the Hawaii Volcanoes National Park headquarters. Check the suitability of your equipment with the rangers, obtain from them the latest information on access and conditions, read this book's description of the Mauna Loa Trail (via Red Hill), and check park literature for more information regarding equipment and hazards.

Drive on Highway 200 (Saddle Road) to the west, about 27 miles from Hilo. Turn off to the south onto a paved road just before reaching Puu Huluhulu, a small but prominent wooded cone to the left of the highway and shortly before the turnoff to Humuula Sheep Station. This road leads for 17 miles through barren lava fields to a weather observatory located at 11,000 feet on the side of Mauna Loa. The road forks about 8 miles from its start. Keep to the paved, right fork. Drive until the observatory comes into view, but park about 300 yards below it where a rough, four-wheel-drive road leads off to the right. No water is available at the trailhead or along the trail.

Follow this road on foot for about 800 yards to the signed trailhead and then follow the *ahu* (rock cairns) and orange-yellow markers, which lead directly up the mountainside on flows of *pahoehoe* (smooth) lava. You will also encounter *aa* (rough) lava on this trail. After about two miles the trail veers somewhat easterly (left) and joins the four-wheel-drive road, passing a locked gate before it leaves to continue more directly up, over ash and *pahoehoe* lava flows. It then recrosses the road and after a considerable climb reaches a junction of trails on the northeast side of North Pit. Periodic lava flows may cover this area and alter the course of the trails. The Summit Trail leads west (right) up to the summit. The Mauna Loa Trail leads northeast, down to Mauna Loa Road via Red Hill. The Cabin Trail (considered here as an extension of the Observatory Trail) leads south across North Pit to Mauna Loa Cabin on the east side of the caldera. Take the Cabin Trail down a short incline to the floor of North Pit. The trail follows *ahu* straight south across the smooth floor of North Pit. It then climbs generally south to the caldera rim, skirting the southwest rim of Lua Poholo, a deep secondary crater. If overtaken by darkness on a clear summer

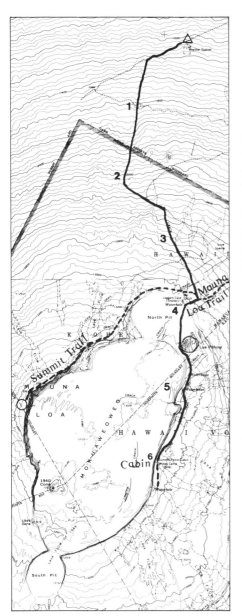

View north to Mauna Kea

sickness more likely on this route. Wear stout boots, preferably expendable ones, for this rough lava. Heavy wool clothing, windbreakers, waterproofs, goggles for snow, sunburn protection, and other mountaineering equipment must be taken. Landmarks are few before reaching the caldera; thus, traveling in uncertain weather or in winter can be perilous and should be avoided.

night, set your course generally on the Southern Cross. Be careful not to fall into Lua Poholo. After passing Lua Poholo, the trail follows along the east rim of the caldera, reaching Mauna Loa Cabin about 1.5 miles past Lua Poholo Crater.

This route is only slightly less difficult physically than the route up from Red Hill, since at these altitudes the thin air makes the miles seem twice as long as at sea level. The rapid gain in elevation makes altitude

9. Akaka Falls
¹/₂ hour, loop trip
50 calories; easiest
0.4 miles, loop trip
Highest point: 1200 feet
Lowest point: 1100 feet
Division of State Parks

This leisurely half-hour hike, suitable for everyone, gives good views of Akaka and Kahuna Falls, two of the more impressive waterfalls in the Hawaiian Islands. The well-maintained trail, with steps in the steeper portions, winds gently down a ridge above the deep canyon into which Akaka and Kahuna Falls plunge. Along the way the trail weaves through dense tropical rain forest replete with epiphytes (non-parasitic plants growing on other plants) hanging from the forest canopy. Brilliant red ginger, fragrant plumeria, banana plants, hapu ferns, ti plants, and the colorful flowers of the bird of paradise make this an especially pleasant hike for a botanist or nature lover. Along the way the Division of State Parks has placed benches as resting places for hikers. You may listen to the muffled roar of the waterfalls in the distance and the occasional sounds of the birds which inhabit this lovely forest.

Akaka Falls

ROUTE: Take Highway 19 north from Hilo and drive about 11 miles to the exit to Akaka Falls State Park on Highway 220. From that junction drive 3.7 miles to the end of the road at the state park, where ample parking is available. Overnight camping is not allowed. You may take the loop trail either clockwise or counterclockwise. If you take it counterclockwise, you will first encounter Kahuna Falls (a *kahuna* was a priest in ancient Hawaii). This beautiful falls cascades from a side canyon across the way into the main canyon below, making several drops into crystal-clear pools. You will next encounter the vista overlooking Akaka Falls (*akaka* means clear or luminous). Kahuna and Akaka Falls resulted from the variations in strength of the underlying layers of rock. The soft, lower layers of rock erode more rapidly than the hard upper layers. As the upper layers are undercut they fall into the pool below, are broken up, and carried away by the plunging waters. In this way, Akaka Falls and others like it have moved upstream over the years.

The trail returns to the parking area through huge philodendrons which stand guard with their 2-foot leaves, making the hiker feel like an insect in the greenery. The top of the trail has well-maintained restrooms, a drinking fountain, and picnic tables with orchids hanging overhead. Even if the weather is poor, this trail is worth taking since the occasional breaks in the mist around the falls only add to the air of beauty and mystery of the location. The dense and wonderfully varying vegetation

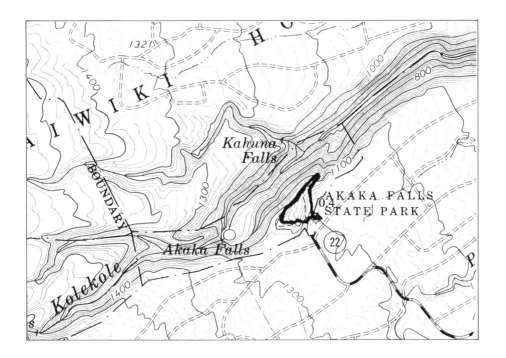

Kahuna Falls

along the trail is in itself a sufficient reason for a visit. In addition the fragrant scents of the rain forest and flowers growing along the trail are much stronger on rainy days.

10. Waipio and Waimanu Valleys (Muliwai Trail)

2-3 days; 9 hours in, 10 hours out
5800 calories; hardest
18 miles, round trip
Highest point: 1350 feet
Lowest point: sea level
Division of Forestry and Wildlife

The Waipio and Waimanu Valleys were centers of Hawaiian civilization in ancient times. Their verdant, well-watered floors supported rich crops of taro which fed a large population. A fertile imagination can conjure up sights of the armies of Kamehameha the Great that once marched in Waipio, the naval battle between the forces of Hawaii and Maui off the Waimanu Valley, and the meetings of the most powerful *kahuna* (ancient Hawaiian priests) in the islands. Some say that human sacrifices were made at a now-vanished *heiau* (a Hawaiian temple) near the mouth of the Waipio Valley. It is even said, somewhat ironically for so beautiful a place, that a tunnel to Hell (now covered with sand) begins somewhere in the valley. Campers must obtain permits from the Division of Forestry and Wildlife.

ROUTE: Drive from Hilo north on Highway 19 for about 42 miles. Turn right onto Highway 240 and follow it through Honokaa for 9.5 miles to the Waipio Valley Lookout, the start of this trail. All cars except four-wheel-drive vehicles must be left at this point since the road down the east slope of the Waipio Valley is very steep. Follow this road down to the valley floor and take the first road to the right all the way to the beach. Wade Wailoa Stream, if safe, close to where it enters the sea. Cross the valley along the beach until you are within 100 yards of the northwest wall. The trail leads up the valley floor past a swampy area into the forest below the northwest wall. A second, faint trail soon intersects from the right. This is the start of the switchback ascent of the northwest wall. The trail, though rough and steep, is less

Headland west of Waimanu Valley

difficult than it looks from the Waipio Valley Lookout since it is well dug into the hillside. Here and elsewhere rain makes the footing slick and hazardous and boots with new tread should be used.

The trail reaches the ridge and contours through numerous small valleys toward the Waimanu Valley. A shelter is located about two-thirds of the way along the trail.

Use care when camping and hiking since there is extreme danger of fire along the trail, especially in the dense pads of needles under the ironwood thickets. The scars of recent forest fires illustrate previous

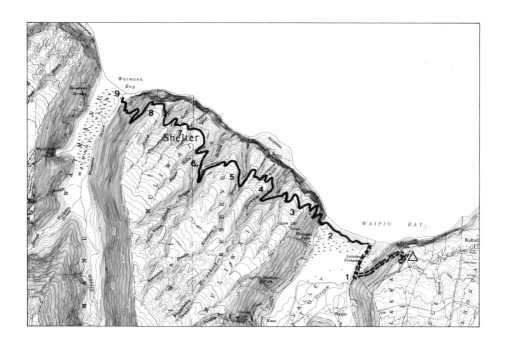

Waipio Valley

carelessness. The trail crosses thirteen low running streams to reach the rim of the Waimanu Valley. During storms these run high and travel should not be attempted.

The Waimanu Valley looks remarkably similar to the Waipio Valley, but it is somewhat smaller and without any human inhabitants. Although covered with loose rock in a few places, the trail down is generally in good shape. At the bottom of the descent, work toward the beach through groves of hala trees. Ford small Waimanu Stream on the southeast end of the beach and follow the beach to the northwest side of the valley. Water from the stream on the

valley floor may be unsafe to drink. Purer water may be obtained from the stream closest to the ocean on the northwest side of the valley; a faint trail leads to it.

A good side trip is to bushwhack up the northwest side of the valley floor through groves of mountain apple trees, laden with tasty fruit, to Waiilikahi Falls and its deep, wide pool. Wild pigs unused to human beings are numerous in this valley and care should be taken not to surprise them. If startled, they may be dangerous. Mosquitoes are plentiful and hungry. Stone walls, foundations, and terraces offer abundant evidence of the ancient civilization.

Island of Maui

Maui's rugged scenery, sheltered beaches, and balmy weather have made it the favorite island of many visitors to the state. The island is formed by two volcanoes, the 10,023-foot-high Haleakala to the east and the 5,788-foot-high West Maui Mountains to the west.

On West Maui the short and easy trail in the Iao Valley gives views of the famous Iao Needle and a great amphitheater valley stream-carved into the ancient caldera. The Waihee Ridge Trail leads up into the West Maui Mountains to give a closer look at the rain forest and remarkable high bog country. The Lahaina Pali Trail, on the dry southern shoulder of the West Maui Mountains, climbs to a view of the great bay formed by Maui, Molokai, Lanai, and Kahoolawe, which were all joined back in geologic time before the islands subsided.

Haleakala Volcano, which forms the east half of the island, is famous for what is popularly called its "crater" and for the remarkable views from the top of the mountain. The "crater" is actually an area formed by two great valleys which coalesced at their heads. The colorful cinder cones and lava flows on the crater floor were created after the valleys were formed. The high crater area is now part of Haleakala National Park, which maintains a network of trails, cabins, and camping areas.

Two long traverses in the park's wilderness area are described here, south-north by the Sliding Sands-Halemauu Trail and west-east by the Sliding Sands-Kaupo Gap Trail. Three cabins are located along these well-marked and well-maintained trails. These trails can be hiked in combination with the many side trails in the crater.

papaya

Haleakala's trails, although not quite as stark as those up Mauna Loa on the island of Hawaii, lead through regions that can be covered with snow at certain times of the year and can at any time be quite wet and cold. Vegetation is sparse; the air is thin. Water is available only at the three strategically located cabins. However, the barrenness of the region makes it all the more interesting, because the great erosion and volcanism that shaped the region are apparent. The little flowers and the fantastic silversword plant that survive in this forbidding landscape are much appreciated

Haleakala Crater

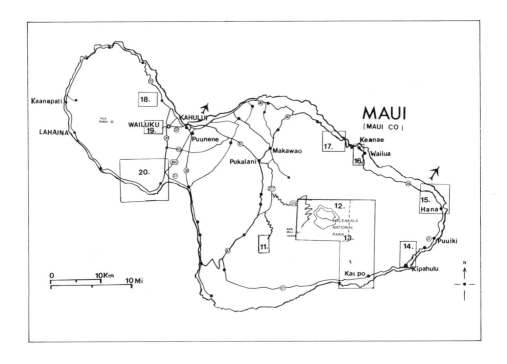

Lava sea cliffs—
Hana-Waianapanapa Coastal Trail

for their efforts.

To use the cabins, be sure to make reservations with Haleakala National Park months in advance. Permits to camp in the crater must be obtained at park headquarters. A maximum of three days for any combination of cabin and campsite use in any one month is allowed. Registration boxes for day hikes are located at the trailheads. Obtain current information from the park regarding your plans.

Haleakala National Park also extends down from the alpine regions at the top of Haleakala to the warm, wet windward coast. The park's Kipahulu Campground on the jagged Hana Coast of the island's windward side and nearby Pipiwai Trail to Waimoku Falls are described in this book. To reach them by road it is necessary to drive all the way around the island on the slow but beautiful Road to Hana.

The Hana Coast of Maui is of special interest to hikers looking for balmy oceanside walking with rocky cliffs, breaking waves, and warm waters. Further inland, trails lead through thick jungles to streams, waterfalls, and pools of rare beauty. Nearby campgrounds provide good bases

Ironwood and naupaka—Hana-Waianapanapa Coastal Trail

for a leisurely tour of these regions. The lush greenery on this side of Maui does have its price; there is much rain. However, the rain is intermittent and warm.

The Polipoli State Park region, high on the southwest side of Haleakala, is comparatively unknown, but offers hiking and camping in the cool, alpine regions of Haleakala. The generally dry lee side weather, pure air and grand views of the island recommend the area. The Division of Forestry and Wildlife has current information and issues camping permits.

The "Polipoli Loop" Trail is centrally located and introduces the area, but there are many more trails. Some of the area's trails wind through now dense stands of redwood, cedar, sugi, and other species imported from more northerly latitudes, providing scenery reminiscent of the west coast of North America. Although many of the region's trails were being steadily destroyed by rooting pigs, now they are being actively upgraded by the agencies in charge of the region. There are several campsites located among the dense stands of redwood and cedar.

You may fly into the regions described in this book via the Kahului or Hana airports and there are direct flights from the mainland of North America. Only small planes land at the Hana airport. Rental cars are available at these airports. Hitchhiking, though illegal, seems to be a popular form of transportation to the hiking areas. The trails on Maui are among the best known in the state, so make reservations well in advance with the appropriate agencies for the use of the cabins described here.

11. Polipoli Loop

3¹/₂ hours, loop trip
800 calories; easier
4.9 miles, loop trip
Highest point: 6200 feet
Lowest point: 5280 feet
Division of State Parks
Division of Forestry and Wildlife

In and near Polipoli State Park is a network of trails, six thousand feet high on the pleasantly cool southwest slope of Haleakala. Central to this network is the "Polipoli Loop" Trail, which consists of parts of the Haleakala Ridge, Plum, and Redwood Trails. The Loop wanders gently through mountainside which was reforested in the 1930's with introduced tree species: pine, Monterey cypress, ash, sugi, red alder, redwood, and several varieties of eucalyptus. These have grown without the influence of the seasons, lighting, and the natural friends and enemies of their distant homelands. Some trees have odd shapes. Others, though apparently growing well, set no seed—perhaps waiting for the triggering cold of a winter that will never come.

Redwood forest— Polipoli Loop

Camping for up to a week is allowed in Polipoli State Park with a permit from the Division of State Parks (P.O. Box 1049, Wailuku, Maui, HI 96793). One cabin, near the campground, is available by reservation. The campground has drinking water. Fires are limited to firepits. Additional trails, much damaged by windfall and pig rooting, are nearby. The elevation makes the area cold in winter and cool at night even in summer. Dress warmly.

ROUTE: Starting at Kahului, take Highway 37 (Haleakala Highway) to Keokea for almost 14 miles to the second turnoff onto Highway 377. Turn left onto Highway 377 and follow it for about 0.4 miles to Waipoli Road.

Turn right and drive up this paved, switchbacking road, which climbs about 3000 feet over a distance of about six miles. It then changes into a maintained gravel road and contours southward about 3.5 miles. Turn right at a fork at almost 10 miles from the start of Waipoli Road and go less than half a mile to the road's end at the Polipoli State Park campground.

The Polipoli Loop Trail starts in a dense stand of Monterey cypress at the campground near the parking area. It contours easily through cypress, cedar, and Monterey pine for 0.6 miles to the Haleakala Ridge Trail, which it joins at multiple points along the upper edge of a grassy area. The loop route follows the Haleakala Ridge Trail to the right, proceeding through stands of eucalyptus, blackwood, swamp mahogany, and hybrid cypress. About 0.4 miles beyond this junction, a short side trail leads left into a cinder cone with a small cave at the bottom.

Less than half a mile after this, there is a

Along the road to Polipoli

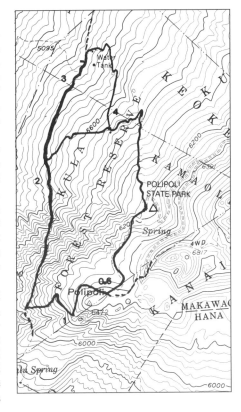

junction where the Haleakala Ridge Trail turns off, left, descending steeply and then soon disappearing. Take the well-travelled Plum Trail contouring right through cool, dense stands of conifers. About a mile from this junction, the Tie Trail leads off uphill (right), to the Redwood Trail, which leads back to the campground. It may be taken as a shortcut.

For the longer route, continue on the Plum Trail for approximately 0.6 miles to a stand of massive redwoods, an old CCC bunkhouse, and a rundown cabin. Camping here is allowed by permit from the Division of State Parks. However, the buildings are in poor condition. Just beyond the cabin, the Plum Trail ends at a junction with the Boundary Trail on the left and the Redwood Trail on the right.

To complete the loop, take the Redwood Trail, which climbs through Mexican pine, tropical ash, Port Orford cedar, and redwood. After 0.9 miles from the previous junction, the upper end of the Tie Trail comes in from the right. The Redwood Trail continues uphill, passing the State Parks rental cabin two hundred yards before reaching the campground.

12. Sliding Sands-Halemauu

2 days; 9 hours, one way
2500 calories; hardest
11.3 miles, one way
Highest point: 9800 feet
Lowest point: 6600 feet
Haleakala National Park

Words cannot adequately describe Haleakala Crater. It must be seen. The expanse of lava flows, vents, cones, and fields of volcanic ash resembles the surface of the moon. It is an awesome, other worldly sight. The Sliding Sands-Halemauu route offers an overnight or a hard one-day trip through the crater, giving a good look at a large part of it. Since the exit on Halemauu Trail is several miles away from and lower than the entrance on the Sliding Sands Trail, located at almost 10,000 feet near the top of Haleakala, arrangements must be made to shuttle between the trailheads. The trip can be made in one day by strong hikers but it is more pleasant to take two days. If you plan to stay in one of the cabins in the crater, confirm your plans with Haleakala National Park three months in advance (P.O. Box 369, Makawao, HI 96768). Camping permits for the back-country camping areas are available on a first-come, first-serve basis at the park headquarters.

Hosmer Grove, located down the road about 4 miles from the trailhead, makes a good base camp, if the trail is to be hiked in one day. The grove was planted in 1910 with many varieties of mainland trees. Native birds flit among their branches. A short nature trail leads from the campground through this mainland forest, passing examples of native plants. Water, a picnic shelter, restrooms, and space for tent camping are available, with no permit or reservation required at present.

Since the weather at these high altitudes can suddenly become cold with high winds and rain or snow, it is necessary to take along boots, waterproofs, warm wool clothes, extra clothes, and, if camping, a

Southwest from Ka Moa o Pele

sleeping bag and a waterproof tent. If one is poorly outfitted and facing the uncertainties of weather, it is best to philosophize that the mountain will still be there and descend back down the road to enjoy Maui's balmy beaches.

ROUTE: Drive from Kahului on Hwy 37 about 10 miles to the turnoff left (east) onto Highway 377 to Haleakala National Park. Follow Highway 377 about 6.5 miles then turn up Haleakala Crater Road (Highway 378). Follow this slow, switchbacking road about 10 miles to the park boundary. At 0.7 miles beyond the park boundary, you will pass Hosmer Grove and

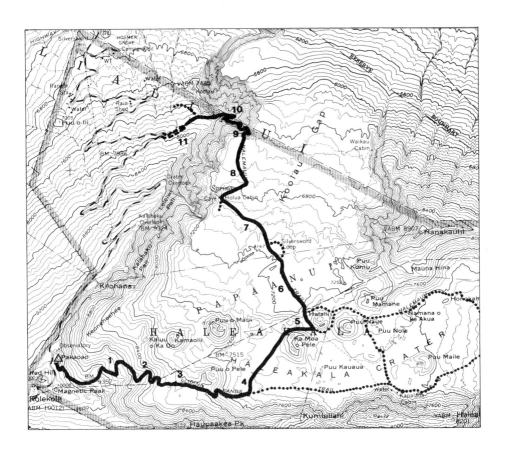

Haleakala Crater—amaumau ferns

shortly thereafter you will reach the park headquarters. Stop at the headquarters for current information regarding camping and hiking. The short turnoff to the exit of the Halemauu Trail is located 4.6 miles past the park boundary. Drive on to the visitor center near the top of Haleakala, 10.6 miles up the road from the park boundary. Day hikers must register for the hike down the Sliding Sands Trail at the box near the Haleakala visitor center. Overnight campers need a permit from the park head-quarters. The trailhead is well marked and the trail is easy to follow as it switchbacks down over talus mantled by ash and cinders onto the crater floor. Resist the temptation to cut the switchbacks since this is a discourtesy to others, causes erosion, and is illegal.

From the descending trail there are good views of the whole crater and the rivers of clouds which flow into the crater through Koolau Gap (to the northeast) and Kaupo Gap (to the east). Vegetation is sparse or absent until one reaches the crater floor. Little bracken ferns, pili grass, shrubs, and flowers begin to appear, increasing in numbers as one travels east. As the trail flattens out it passes a cinder cone, Puu o Pele (Hill of Pele), off to the left (north). The trail then begins another, moderately steep descent to the crater floor beyond Puu o Pele. At the end of this descent and almost at the four-mile point the Sliding Sands Trail is joined by a connecting trail leading northeast a mile and a half across the crater floor to the Halemauu Trail. The Sliding Sands Trail leads straight ahead, east, reaching Kapalaoa Cabin after 1.8 miles and Paliku Cabin after 5.8 miles from this junction.

Take the connecting trail, left (north), toward the left shoulder of Ka Moa o Pele, a red and black cinder cone toward the center of the crater. The trail leads across relatively flat, ash-covered flows of basalt, then climbs up the cinder-covered side of Ka Moa o Pele to a saddle between it and an older cone adjacent to the north. The saddle is one of the best places in the crater for taking pictures of the colorful landscape and impressive cones to the west. Nearby grow fine examples of the silversword. Use care to stay several feet away since their delicate feeder roots lie just below the sur-rounding cinders.

Silversword

Moonscape

Nene goose

The trail descends to the saddle between Ka Moa o Pele and Halalii cinder cone to the northeast. The trail skirts a small, narrow flow of dark gray basaltic *pahoehoe* (smooth) lava called "Pele's Pig Pen." At Pele's Pig Pen it joins the trail circling Halalii. Here one can go right, circling the cone to its northeast side, or go left, northwest. Take care not to take the trail to Kapalaoa, as it branches to the right (southeast) a short distance beyond Pele's Pig Pen. Either route around Halalii ends up on the Halemauu Trail. Just as the route to the right joins the Halemauu Trail, it passes "the Bottomless Pit," a deep volcanic vent. As Halemauu Trail continues on to the north of Halalii it passes a colorful spatter cone area called "Pele's Paint Pot." The route to the left misses these but saves about half a mile of travel.

Once the Halemauu Trail is reached, follow it west and north across a barren moonscape of ash and lava to Holua cabin, which lies 1.9 miles from the northwest flank of Halalii. Midway to the cabin the trail passes the Silversword Loop. This half-mile loop provides good views of silverswords.

The Halemauu Trail gradually climbs out of the deepest ash as it passes the Silversword Loop and moves onto red, then black lava with firmer footing and increasing vegetation, including kukaenene, pukeiawe, and evening primrose. It slowly descends for a mile before reaching Holua Cabin. The cabin and nearby water tank sit above the trail near the crater wall. A tent camping area (by permit) is located about 200 yards south of the cabin. Open fires are not permitted anywhere in the crater. Be courteous and do not disturb those who have rented the cabins.

From Holua Cabin the trail goes generally north, down the lava, and across a meadow to the switchbacks leading back up the crater wall. From the meadow the trail climbs a twisting, lovely course to gain over a thousand feet to the crater rim. Hikers should be sure to step aside and stand quietly next to the trail to let horses pass by. Along the way one may see a handsome display of the red and green amaumau ferns. At length the top of the wall is reached and the trail climbs gradually through hinahina and other native Hawaiian plants to the start of the road somewhat over a mile away, passing a side trail going downhill to Hosmer Grove along the way.

13. Sliding Sands-Kaupo Gap
2-3 days; 13-14 hours, one way
5300 calories; hardest
17.5 miles, one way
Highest point; 9800 feet
Lowest point: 250 feet
Haleakala National Park

This is the grand tour of Haleakala Crater, traversing its entire length from west to east and descending through Kaupo Gap to the sea coast: a total drop of almost 10,000 feet in about 18 miles. It has the advantage of being nearly all downhill, but the disadvantage that transportation must be provided at the lower end to avoid a monumental return trip.

Haleakala Crater was formed by two great valleys, Koolau and Kaupo. Erosion caused these to join together and widen at their heads. Subsequent volcanic activity covered the area with lava and cinder cones leaving a barren and beautiful landscape.

The trail starts out at nearly 10,000 feet, where the air is clear and the view immense. A wide-angle lens is useful because of the scale of the scenery. The crater can be very windy, wet, and cold. Therefore, it is necessary to take boots, waterproofs, warm wool clothes, extra clothes, tents, and sleeping bags. The weather is remarkably changeable in the crater. It is possible to suffer from both severe sunburn and hypothermia on the same day. If unprepared, one should avoid this hike.

Two cabins, Kapalaoa and Paliku, are located along this route. If you plan to stay in these you must make reservations three months in advance with Haleakala National Park. Water is usually available at tanks next to the cabins. Camping is not permitted near Kapalaoa, but a tent camping area is located 200 yards from Paliku Cabin. Camping permits for Poliku Campground are available at the park headquarters on a first-come, first-serve basis. To preserve the area, open fires are forbidden.

ROUTE: Drive to Haleakala National Park

West of Kapalaoa Cabin

headquarters. Stop to obtain the latest information regarding conditions and permits. Go 10.5 miles to the visitor center near the top of Haleakala. The trail begins near the center and is well marked as the "Sliding Sands Trail," the only apparent route down the slopes into the crater. Day hikers must sign in.

Follow the Sliding Sands Trail down to Kapalaoa Cabin, located about 5.8 miles from the trailhead and 4.0 miles from Paliku Cabin. If you have arranged to stay overnight at Kapalaoa Cabin instead of proceeding directly to Paliku, it is worthwhile to explore some of the short trails leading north from the cabin to various points of interest. From Kapalaoa Cabin proceed east down the well-marked trail to join the Halemauu Trail. Continue east (right) down the Halemauu Trail, passing

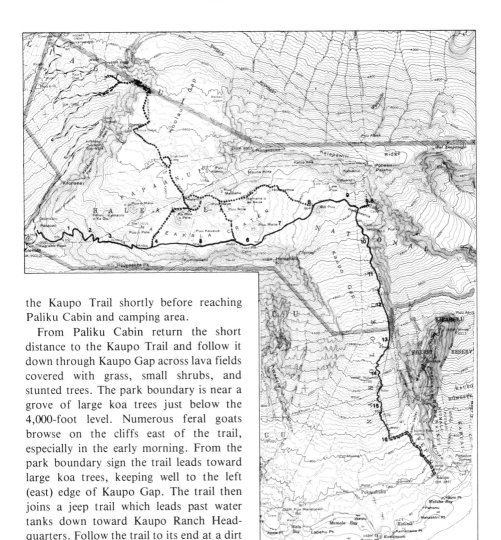

the Kaupo Trail shortly before reaching Paliku Cabin and camping area.

From Paliku Cabin return the short distance to the Kaupo Trail and follow it down through Kaupo Gap across lava fields covered with grass, small shrubs, and stunted trees. The park boundary is near a grove of large koa trees just below the 4,000-foot level. Numerous feral goats browse on the cliffs east of the trail, especially in the early morning. From the park boundary sign the trail leads toward large koa trees, keeping well to the left (east) edge of Kaupo Gap. The trail then joins a jeep trail which leads past water tanks down toward Kaupo Ranch Headquarters. Follow the trail to its end at a dirt road just below the ranch headquarters. This dirt road leads down to the coastal road (Highway 31, the "King's Highway," or the Piilani Highway).

Drivers meeting you at the trail's end must either drive the dry, barren coastal road east from Ulupalakua or drive west from Hana for about 17 miles on the scenic but rough coastal road. The road from Ulupalakua is usually in better condition, closed less often by washouts, and a shorter distance from central Maui than the road from Hana. A good landmark for the turn-off to the side leading up to the trailhead is a picturesque seaside church 0.5 miles east of the turnoff. Kaupo is located just west of the turnoff. Since there is little to amuse those waiting at the trail's end, and the

coastal road to Hana is spectacular, hikers could walk down to the road and along it east about nine miles to the Haleakala National Park's Oheo Campground and the Waimoku Falls area (described in this book).

An alternative to the hike to the seacoast from Poliku Cabin is to hike back up the crater via the Halemauu Trail located on the north side of the crater (described earlier in this book). Holua Cabin is 6.3 miles from Paliku Cabin via this interesting route, which eliminates the difficult problem of arranging transportation from the sea coast.

14. Pipiwai (Waimoku Falls)

3-4 hours, round trip
1050 calories, easier
4 miles, round trip
Highest point: 1000 feet
Lowest point: 150 feet
Haleakala National Park

This is an area of swimming holes and waterfalls of remarkable beauty where the ancient Hawaiians lived, fished, farmed, and swam. The pools have long been considered one of the most attractive areas on Maui. The federal government recognized the area's beauty and preserved it as a part of Haleakala National Park. The inevitable result of such fame and recognition is that the lovely pools near the road can be crowded. Fortunately, other attractive areas exist upstream. The lack of crowds there reflects a natural law first formulated by Professor Joel Hildebrand. According to Hildebrand's Law the number of people in a wilderness area diminishes in proportion to the square of the distance and the cube of the elevation from the nearest road. Thus, the upper areas are reserved for those willing to walk. The trail to the upper areas leads to a viewpoint overlooking Makahiku Falls and to Waimoku Falls farther up the valley.

ROUTE: From Hana, on the east end of Maui, follow Highway 31 southwest 10 miles to a small bridge crossing Oheo Gulch. A parking area is located less than a quarter of a mile past the bridge. A short, well-maintained trail parallels the southwest side of the stream, providing good views of the pools below the bridge. Avoid viewing from the narrow, heavily traveled bridge. The pools below the bridge provide good swimming, though there is the possibility of flash floods. The ocean currents are dangerous and local sharks are reputed to have developed a taste for warm meat. The Waimoku Falls Trail begins across the road from the parking area. Proceed directly up the hillside, following the obvious trail

Waimoku Falls Trail

which roughly parallels the course of Oheo Stream. The track forks about 800 paces from its begining; the right fork goes 50 paces to the brink of a cliff overlooking Makahiku Falls. After regaining the main trail follow it up through pasture toward the head of the valley. There the trail drops steeply down a bank, through guava, mango, and Christmas-berry, to reach Palikea Stream. The trail crosses the stream just above a small pool into which two small waterfalls plunge.

The trail then climbs the bank of Palikea Stream, leads through guava and thickets of bamboo, past overgrown taro patches, over small boardwalks, and through a nar-

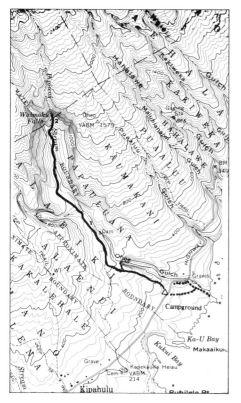

row corridor in a final thicket of bamboo. On the far side of the corridor the trail comes to Pipiwai Stream and turns left. It then closely follows the bank of the stream about 300 paces to its confluence with another stream from the left. Shortly after the confluence, the trail crosses the left-hand stream and proceeds up the right-hand stream to Waimoku Falls, about 250 paces beyond the confluence. Avoid swimming in or crossing these streams during high water. If the water level rises, get out fast; upstream rains can create dangerous flashfloods.

The national park's Oheo Campground is located along a dirt road leading a half mile seaward from the parking area. This waterless campground is quite large and sits on a spectacular, mosquito-free location above Kukui Bay. The closest supply of potable water is in Hana. Waianapanapa State Park, described under the Hana-Waianapanapa Coastal Trail, is also a good location for tent camping (by permit). Make reservations months in advance to use the cabins in the state park.

Oheo Gulch — falls and plunge pool

15. Hana-Waianapanapa Coastal Trail

4 hours, round trip
700 calories; easier
6 miles, round trip
Highest point: 40 feet
Lowest point: sea level
Division of State Parks

Waianapanapa State Park is set in a wooded location between Hana airport and the small community of Hana beside two pebbly, little beaches on Pailoa Bay. Reservations for the rental cabins at the campground must be made months in advance. Picnic tables, showers, tent sites, and restroom facilities are available.

The coastal trail next to the campground is a jewel among coastal trails in the state. It parallels the sea along small lava cliffs formed by the action of the waves on recent flows and is bounded inland by a dense forest of hala trees. The play of light in the early morning or late evening on the dark, textured lava and the light surf makes the area especially suited for black and white photography. At midday the light is flat and the trail can be too warm, with little shade and no potable water.

In addition to its beauty, the trail has historic interest since it follows the ancient Hawaiian "King's Highway" paralleling Maui's seacoast. Smooth, water-worn stepping stones placed on the jagged lava to soften the trail for the feet of travelers mark this ancient Hawaiian trail. The kings of the island and their retainers following the trail would come to collect taxes from the various districts. The stones are so old that rain water has eroded many of them. Not far from the park the trail passes an ancient *heiau* (temple) and several building foundations. The remarkable flower called beach naupaka flourishes along the trail. Its blossoms appear to have but half a flower; a related species with only half a flower is found in the mountains. This peculiarity has given rise to many legends. One relates that the gods, tiring of the quarrels of two

Naupaka

lovers, turned them into these distinctive flowers and condemned them to live apart, one in the mountains and one by the sea.

ROUTE: Coming from the north on the Hana Highway (360), go 0.6 miles past the Hana Airport turnoff to the Waianapanapa Campground turnoff on the left (seaward). Proceed down this narrow, paved, two-lane road to the campground. The trail can be joined at any point between the campground and the sea since it extends along the coast in both directions. The portion going toward Hana is the longer and more interesting, first passing a blowhole and then the ruins of a *heiau.* The trail ends at Kainalimu Bay.

The portion of the trail north of the campground goes by two small, pleasant beaches, Pailoa and Keawaiki, and then leads on to the rough lava country close to the airport. The terrain becomes less interesting after leaving the beaches and progressively more rugged.

Waianapanapa Cave is a nearby feature of historic interest, reached by a short trail just west of the campground. Here a queen of Maui sought refuge from victorious enemies by swimming underwater to a hidden portion of the cave. To her misfortune, a faint trail of blood revealed the hiding place to her pursuers, who killed her.

The "King's Highway"

16. Keanae Arboretum

1-2 hours, round trip
400 calories; easiest
3 miles, round trip
Highest point: 400 feet
Lowest point: 160 feet
Division of Forestry and Wildlife

The easy trail through Keanae Arboretum Trail, in lush windward Maui, offers a first-hand view of paddy taro cultivation and rare native Hawaiian plants. Taro is generally grown in paddies washed by fresh-flowing streams. It was the most important food crop of the original Hawaiians since it is immensely productive. Some say that as many as 300,000 Hawaiians lived in the Hawaiian Islands in pre-contact times, fed by taro. The figure is believable since evidence of taro cultivation is found any place in the Hawaiian Islands that could support taro, even in the remotest areas.

Taro leaves, even older ones, show little sign of insect damage—without application of pesticide. Nature has already done the job by adding to the plant calcium oxalate crystals which sting predators, making taro almost immune to the depredations of insects and animals. Thorough cooking destroys the crystals and makes taro safe to eat. Poi, the staple of the original Hawaiians' diet, is made from taro roots. All parts are edible. The young leaves of the plant provided the substance of several nourishing dishes. Less desireable parts could be fed to pigs.

ROUTE: Drive east on Highway 360 from Kahului approximately 47 miles to a sharp turn in the road 0.1 miles after the Keanae YMCA Camp and just before the turnoff to Keanae. Parking is available next to a large sign indicating Keanae Arboretum. A gate blocks traffic down the paved ramp to the arboretum. The trail, following the course of the dirt road in the arboretum, first passes through planted groves of trees. Labels give the names of

Pool on Piinaau Stream

various species, such as hibiscus, cashew nut, grapefruit, citrus paradisi, royal palm, and Cook pine.

The trail then reaches the irrigated taro patches. Finally, it goes up into the rain forest and crosses a tributary stream. From this point the trail is unmaintained and may become too hard to follow. If so, simply retrace your steps. This portion of the trail, such as it is, does give a notion of the type of forest to be found in this part of the island.

The area is wet, so expect rain—and mosquitoes. Beware of flash flooding along the creek. The best overnight tent camping in the area (by permit) is located at Waianapanapa State Park near Hana. To use the cabins at the park, make reservations months in advance.

Taro patches

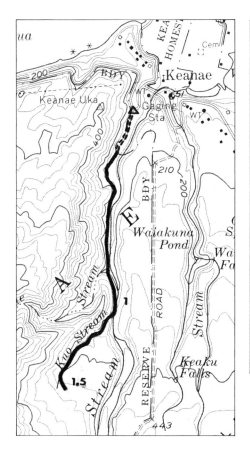

17. Waikamoi Ridge Loop

1 hour, loop trip
150 calories; easiest
1 mile, loop trip
Highest point: 800 feet
Lowest point: 630 feet
Division of Forestry and Wildlife

The Waikamoi Ridge Loop Trail climbs to a hilltop shelter and picnic area in an area reforested during the 1930's with paper bark and eucalyptus. This loop trail is in good shape. An undergrowth of ferns of various sorts, mushrooms, and ti plants adds variety.

Stone benches thoughtfully placed along the route provide pleasant rest stops. Mosquitoes are less plentiful here than in streamside areas. They do not like exposure to the trades and sunshine near the hilltop shelter. Thus, this is a good place for a picnic along the Hana road. No water is available and camping is not permitted here.

ROUTE: Take Highway 360, the road to Hana, 3.5 miles past Kailua. The trailhead is 9.6 miles along the highway as measured by the mileage markers, on the uphill side of the road. There is ample room for parking. A picnic shelter, for the less energetic, is located in a stand of large eucalyptus. Two main trails lead from it. One goes left, paralleling the road. This is the return leg of the loop and can be ignored for the time being.

Take the trail leading fairly directly up the hill. It ascends through paperbark and large eucalyptus covered with climbing philodendrons. Tree roots provide good footing on the wet trail, creating a stairstep effect. The trail passes by ti plants and large ferns as it switchbacks up to gain the ridge.

At a junction on the ridgeline, note the return leg of the loop leading, left, down the ridge. A nearby stone bench offers a rest and a view of a bamboo-covered valley and the road to Hana below. Continue up and contour right to join a jeep road in a few minutes. Turn left up the jeep road.

Eucalyptus forest

The grassy picnic area and the hilltop shelter come into view almost immediately.

The trail's end is a good picnic spot for a family. There is ample room for small children to romp under the watchful eyes of their parents. The view of the surrounding hills, though not breathtaking, is pleasant. The trade winds sigh in the trees.

Return the way you came until you reach the junction where you noted the return leg of the loop going down the ridge. Follow it back to the roadside shelter and the trailhead to complete the loop. Do not return via the jeep road, since it is slippery and muddy.

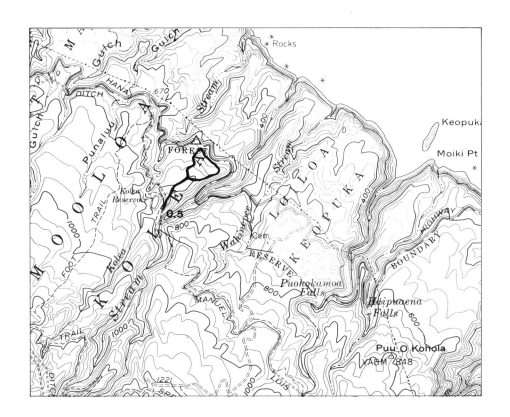

Picnic area

18. Waihee Ridge

3½ hours, round trip
900 calories; harder
4.5 miles, round trip
Highest point: 2563
Lowest point: 1050
Division of Forestry and Wildlife

West Maui's valleys, deeper and more rugged than East Maui's, show that erosion has had a longer time to work without interruption by volcanic building. The Waihee Ridge Trail leads up onto a ridge above such deep valleys, offering spectacular scenery. Waihee Ridge, preserved from erosion by exceptionally durable lava, climbs gradually from pasture land and guava thickets up into wetter areas of West Maui where there is still much native vegetation. There are fine views of the waterfalls in the Makamakaole Valley, the Waihee Valley, central Maui, and, finally, Mount Eke. There is no drinkable water along the route, but the trail is well-marked and in good shape. Choose a dry day.

ROUTE: Drive northwest about four miles from Wailuku along the coastline to Waihee. Continue from Waihee Elementary School 2.7 miles farther northwest, to a paved turnoff, on the left, leading to the Boy Scouts' Camp Maluhia. Turn there and drive up 0.9 miles. The trailhead is at a parking area on the left side of the road, before reaching the Scout camp, and is probably marked by a brown "Na Ala Hele" sign. Go through the cattle fence at the first of three stiles, designed, no doubt, in Hell's seventh circle for the torment of gluttons.

A right of way easement leads for 0.3 miles straight southwest up the hill through private pasturage to the boundary of the West Maui Forest Reserve, which is marked by a fence with a second narrow stile. Note the differences in vegetation delineated by the fence. Beyond the fence the shady path, which is also a dirt road, is flanked by planted Norfolk Island pine on the left and invading guava on the right. The road soon disappears as the trail swings right to sidehill up the slope. Just as the trail turns left on a switchback, there is a fine view of a double waterfall in the Makamakaole Valley, to the north.

The trail continues a switchbacking ascent along the ridgeline, passing good views of the deep Waihee Valley, Mount Eke, waterfalls, and central Maui across to Haleakala. At about 1.6 miles the trail rounds a corner, passes between Norfolk Island pine, and comes to a small, open swampy area. The trail crosses it and switchbacks up to the top of Lanilili. Note and avoid the deep sinkholes along the trail climbing up Lanilili. The trail ends at the two and a quarter mile mark, a good place for a picnic.

There are fine views of Mt. Eke to the southwest and down to wild rain-soaked peat swamps, forested ridges, and steep valleys of the West Maui Natural Area Reserve, Kahakuloa Section.

Return as you came.

Waihee Valley

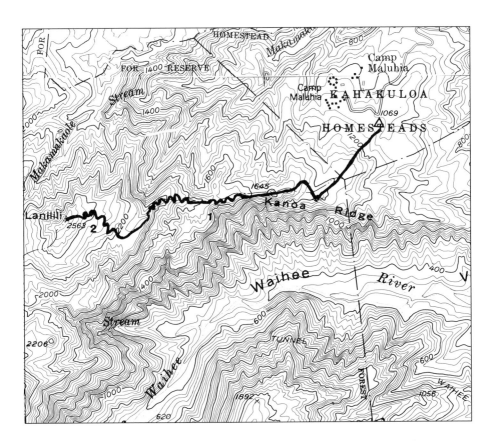

19. Iao Valley

¹/₂ hour, loop trip
50 calories; easiest
0.3 miles, loop trip
Highest point: 1080 feet
Lowest point: 950 feet
Division of State Parks

Iao Stream has cut a deep, narrow gorge from Wailuku into the heart of the West Maui Mountains, providing one of the few easy access routes to a close view of this region. A paved road follows the stream course up the valley, ending at Iao Valley State Park and the famous Iao Needle. Beyond them the valley widens into a massive, green amphitheater, ringed by fluted cliffs and topped by perpetual rain clouds.

At the back of the amphitheater, which was once occupied by West Maui's central caldera, is 5788-foot-high, rain-drenched, Puu Kukui, the highest point on West Maui. The short, paved trail winding through Iao Valley State Park, free of the customary staining mud, offers a gentleman's walk to views of the needle and the streams crossing the area through lush vegetation.

Of interest on the road to the park from Wailuku is Hale Hoikeike, "the Bailey House," carefully preserved as an historical museum by the Maui Historical Society. Kepaniwai County Park, half a mile down the valley from the State Park, is notable for its pavilions constructed in the styles of various Pacific Rim peoples. As a side trip one may pick a path to wander among them. In 1790 Kalanikupule, chief of Maui, is said to have made a stand here during a bloody retreat from Kamehameha's invading army.

Hawai'i Nature Center, a hands-on, non-profit environmental education center, next to the upper end of Kepaniwai County Park, offers programs for school children, guided interpretive hikes to areas requiring special permission, classes, and nature crafts. These are open to the public with

Iao Needle

advance registration.

ROUTE: From downtown Wailuku take Main Street toward the mountains. Pass Hale Hoikeike and later veer right at a fork down into the Iao Valley. The road soon passes Tropical Gardens of Maui, with its pleasant pathways and extraordinary collection of orchids. Just after Kepaniwai Park there is a gate which is closed at night. The road ends at a parking area. The

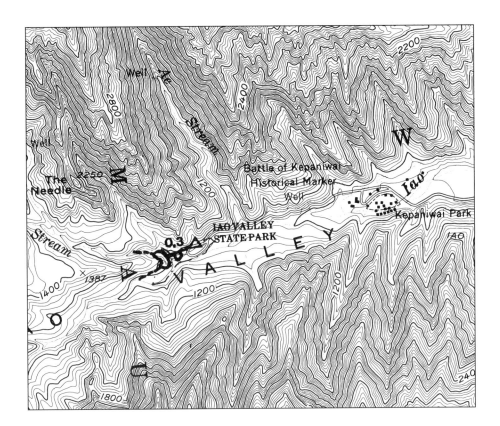

paved trail through the park starts nearby
the restrooms and soon takes a footbridge
over a stream. Just before the footbridge,
the trail passes above a nature loop with
labelled plants, which is worth a brief side
trip. The path after footbridge leads to a
junction. Keep right and go to another
fork, where a spur climbs to a shelter with
a fine view of the Iao Needle. A rough trail
of use leads from behind the lookout up
onto a plateau in the valley, but is on private land.

Return to the junction below the lookout
and descend, right, for a pleasant streamside return. The muddy trails of use that
leave the paved trail to go up the stream
are on private land. The paved trail down
soon turns toward the footbridge to complete the loop.

20. Lahaina Pali Trail

4 hours, one-way
900 calories, harder
5.5 miles, one-way
Highest point: 1640 feet
Lowest point: 100 feet
Division of Forestry and Wildlife

The Lahaina Pali Trail is Maui's demonstration trail under Na Ala Hele, Hawaii's trail and access system. Opened in 1993, it follows the course of an old Hawaiian trail, which was improved to provide a horseback route from the isthmus area between East and West Maui over to the Lahaina side of the island.

Overland transit in Hawaii usually presents problems because of deep valleys that cut into the mountains and cliffs that border the sea. A drive around the southern side of West Maui demonstrates the obstacles in the terrain, now solved by modern engineering. The Lahaina Pali Trail avoided these difficulties by cutting over the shoulder of the mountain, climbing just enough to pass above the cliffs of Manawainui Gulch.

Though the trail is not technically difficult, it is a long climb and is best taken in the cool of the day. The land has been long overgrazed, but there are some native plants in the upper regions. From the higher parts of the trail there are fine views of Lanai, Kahoolawe, Maalaea Bay and, from November to April, of humpback whales. Since the trail is waterless and can be warm, it may be a good plan to combine the hike with a swim at Ukumehame Beach Park, a shady spot near the trailhead.

ROUTE: The trailhead is on Highway 30, three miles west of Maalaea Harbor and ten miles southeast of Lahaina near the 11-mile marker. It is about one quarter of a mile northwest of the tunnel, towards Lahaina, on Highway 30. Park at the interpretive sign at the pull-off on the mauka (mountain) side of the road. The trail goes inland, crosses the abandoned old highway, goes up it a hundred yards then climbs the old highway bank to reach the historic trail.

The trail climbs steadily. At first the route is out of the cooling trade winds, though these are felt with much relief at about the 1000-foot level. Rocks along the way have been written upon by travelers long ago in the blocky script of the 1800's. The trail crosses Manawainui Gulch at the 1350-foot level. Then it joins a 4-wheel drive trail coming up from near McGregor Point, the view improves and there is more vegetation.

The trail climbs somewhat and then crosses Malalowaiaole Gulch at almost three miles from the start of the trail. Soon after this, at an elevation of about 1600 feet, the old trail leaves the 4-wheel drive road and begins its descent toward the flat lowland. With fine views of Maalaea Boat Harbor, Maalaea Bay, and East Maui, this is a good turnaround place for those unable to arrange for a ride at the end of the trail.

If a ride can be arranged, a one-way, complete traverse of the shoulder is feasible. To continue, follow the Lahaina Pali Trail leading down and northeast to a roadside trailhead two and a half miles away.

Watching for humpback whales, Kahoolawe in the distance

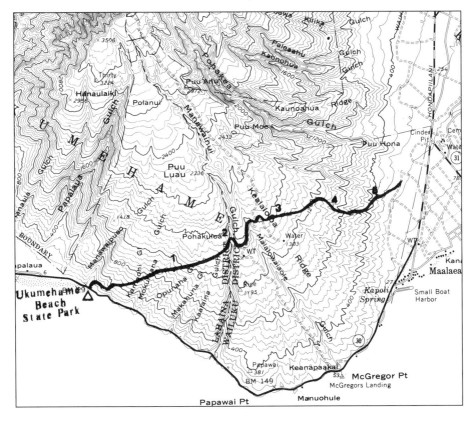

Islands of Lanai and Molokai

Both Lanai and Molokai, together with dry and lonely Kahoolawe, were once joined to Maui. Subsidence created an inland sea ringed by these islands, used more than a century ago as a roadstead for wintering sailing ships. It is now a playground for sailboats and parasailors. Boats ferry passengers from Lahaina on West Maui to Manele Harbor on the south coast of Lanai, and aircraft link the islands' airfields by short hops.

The island of Lanai was formed by one shield volcano. Its central caldera is now the cool, upland site of Lanai City. To its east is what remains of the rim of the caldera, the 3370-foot-high summit ridge of Lanaihale.

Cook Island pines - Lanai

The Munro Trail traverses the length of the rim of the old caldera, past deep gorges and through pleasant wooded areas. It offers excellent views of Molokai, Maui, and Kahoolawe. A four-wheel-drive road leads down to the northwest shore of Lanai, where long and uncrowded Polihua Beach offers some of the best beach walking in the Hawaiian Islands.

Lanai, nearly all privately owned, provides an example of early conservation efforts to overcome the damage of overgrazing. Lanai once supported a substantial population and was covered with native vegetation. Overgrazing made the island virtually a desert. Later owners of Lanai, including most recently Castle and Cooke, made commendable efforts to halt the erosion and destruction of the island's watershed.

Wild livestock were destroyed and imported trees and grasses were planted to hold the soil. Stands of eucalyptus, tall rows of Cook Island pine, and a gradually advancing forest illustrate the long-term results of the policy. More recently, the corporation generously placed a portion of the island containing rare, native dryland forest under a conservation easement to the Nature Conservancy of Hawaii.

The island is no longer devoted to pineapple. Instead it has been developed as a luxury resort destination. The Lodge at Koele in the uplands near Lanai City and Manele Bay Hotel on Hulopoe Beach are two of the finest hotels in the Hawaiian Islands. Guided hikes to a number of areas are available to guests of the hotels. There are also daily meals and a small number of rooms available at Hotel Lanai, a most charming and authentic part of old Hawaii.

Camping, with tents, is available only at Hulopoe Beach. The pleasant campground, with water and facilities, is maintained by Lanai Company, from whom reservations need to be obtained. A rental car is needed for transportation on the island.

The island of Molokai, the northernmost of this island group, is composed of two

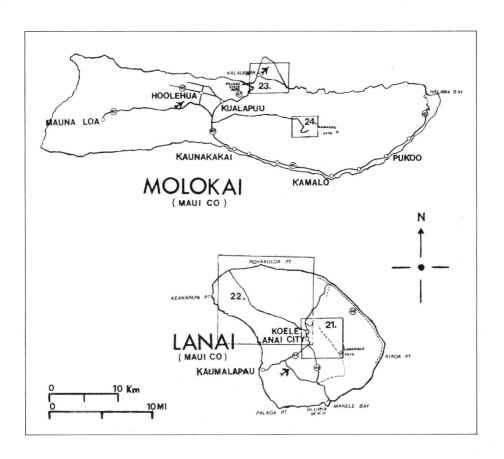

View from Lanai to East Molokai

Garden of the Gods on the way to Polihua Beach

North Coast — Molokai

major volcanoes: one on the east and one on the west. Only the eastern volcano is high enough to stop the trade winds and wring water from them to nourish bogs and forests and create streams and waterfalls. This book describes two trails on East Molokai.

The Kalaupapa Trail, on the North Coast, starts near the isolated Paalau State Park. The trail descends the precipitous face of a great scarp to a low shield volcano, offering fine views of immense sea cliffs. In Palau State Park, a short trail leads from the campground to nearby Phallic Rock.

The Pepeopae Trail leads by boardwalk through the Nature Conservancy of Hawaii's Pepeopae Bog Preserve, 4000 feet above the North Coast of Molokai. It is accessible via a four-wheel-drive Molokai Forest Reserve road leading in from the west off Highway 46. Along the way the road passes the Sandalwood Pit and a grand view of Waikolu Valley.

Several reasonable hotels in Kaunakakai, on the southern coast, provide lodging and food. A destination resort in the western-most part of Molokai is located on one of the most delightful beaches in Hawaii.

Visitor transportation around the island of Molokai is generally by rental car or hitch-hiking (though illegal). There is no public transportation.

21. Munro Trail

7 hours, round trip
2050 calories; harder
11 miles, round trip
Highest point: 3370 feet
Lowest point: 1950 feet
Lanai Company

The Munro Trail is named for George Munro, who carried out the reforestation of the Island of Lanai in the early 1900's. Just as he planned many years ago, the seedling Norfolk Island pines planted along the tops of ridges are now large trees, collecting water directly from mists borne on the trade winds. As the mists pass over the high ridges, tiny water droplets accumulate on the needles until large drops form and fall to earth.

The trees steadily accumulate great quantities of water for the island and support the returning vegetation around them. Note the permanent puddles of water at the base of each tree. This process, called "fog drip," accounts for "rain" forests (actually low cloud forests) in temperate areas whose rainfall alone is too light to support such forests.

It is said that Munro first observed this phenomenon on the large Norfolk Island pine that grew next to his ranch home at Koele. Pictures from the turn of the century show what an overgrazed, desert waste Lanai once was. Munro's thought, modest investment of effort, and the passage of time have grown to a rich legacy indeed.

The Munro Trail, which follows what is left of the rim of Lanai's ancient caldera, was expanded from an access horse trail into a rough jeep trail. It also serves as an easy-to-follow foot trail from the drier areas of the island through the heart of the forested areas and over the highest point on Lanai, Lanaihale, at 3,370 feet. On a clear day it provides fine views of the Islands of Molokai, Maui, Hawaii, Kahoolawe, and even Oahu. The visibility is usually best in the morning.

The trail is useable by the permission of Lanai Company, but does pass through hunting areas. Check with Lanai Company in Lanai City before the hike and wear bright clothing.

ROUTE: Go north from Lanai City along Keomoku Road (Highway 44) for 1.5 miles almost to a low pass. Here turn right onto a paved road which leads in 0.2 miles to the Lanai cemetery. Measure distance from this turn, the start of the hike. Near the cemetery the road veers somewhat left to contour below the golf course, then in and out of eucalyptus covered gullies. Near Maunalei Gulch it passes a short side road to the left, then begins a long uphill climb and becomes more of a trail than a road.

About 3 miles from the start, the trail passes Hookio Gulch, a branch of Maunalei Gulch. The ridge between the gulches, marked by three notches, was the last refuge of fleeing Lanai islanders who were attacked by Kalaniopuu's army from the Island of Hawaii in 1778. The defenders were reduced by thirst and starvation and then massacred.

About 4.0 miles along the Munro Trail there is a fine viewpoint of Lanai City and the ancient caldera. This is a good turn-around point for a shorter hike. The Munro Trail reaches Lanaihale, the highest point on Lanai, in another 1.3 miles. This is the endpoint for this description. Return as you came. The trail goes on to make a long descent to the south of the island leading to a dirt road crossing fields and eventually reaching the highway from Lanai City to Manele Bay.

Fog drip puddle beneath Norfolk Island pine

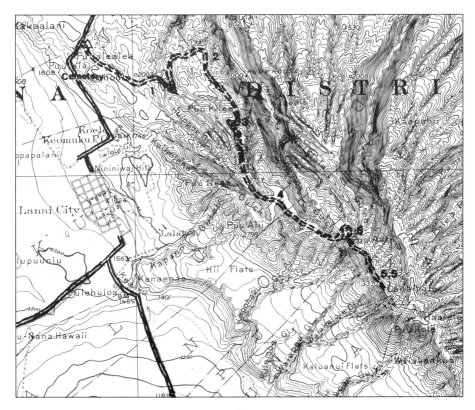

22. Polihua Beach

3-4 hours, round trip
460 calories; easier
3-4 miles, round trip
Highest point: sea level
Lowest point: sea level
The Lanai Company, Inc.

This easy hike offers beach combing in the Hawaiian Islands at its best. Hawaiian beaches have much variety: red cinder, black lava fragments, green olivine crystals, and white coral. This beach is, perhaps, the prettiest of all, consisting of highly polished fragments of sea shells and coral. Innumerable tiny sea shells, still intact, line the shore. Glass balls and other treasures are sometimes washed ashore. The Island of Molokai lying only a few miles away across Kalohi Channel is clearly visible during the entire length of the hike. On a weekday, this long, wide beach is usually deserted, leaving you to beachcomb or contemplate in solitude.

Polihua Road, the steep and rough road leading to the beach, requires a 4-wheel-drive vehicle. Extra water should be carried since the trip can be hot and no water is available along the route. Since the 10-mile road to the beach has little traffic, carry appropriate supplies and leave word of your route. Check with the rangers at Lanai Company to find out if there will be hunters in the area.

ROUTE: Starting from the center of Lanai City drive northerly past the Lodge at Koele. Take the first left onto a dirt road leading down past the stables. Continue to an intersection with another dirt road and turn right. Follow the road through fairly flat land covered with high grass. At about five miles it reaches Kanepuu Preserve. Kanepuu Preserve is a rare native dryland forest placed under the stewardship of the Nature Conservancy of Hawaii by Lanai Company.

After about a mile past the Preserve, Kaena Road enters from the left. Continue past it. The main road soon reaches an extremely eroded area where rocks of bizarre shapes and colors are exposed. This is referred to as the

White sands, seashells and coral

Garden of the Gods. Before the introduction of grazing animals in the 1800's, these lands had deep soil and native dryland forests. The endemic plants had evolved without adaptations to withstand grazing and were quickly destroyed by goats and cattle. The soil, once exposed to the elements, was quickly eroded and swept down to the coast, in some places moving the coastline out to sea.

The road begins a 5-mile, 1700-foot descent to Polihua Beach and, as it reaches the beach, the road forks. Take the turnoff to the right which ends shortly at the beach. There, begin your hike. There is no specific trail; simply follow the beautiful sandy beach as far as is feasible, and return.

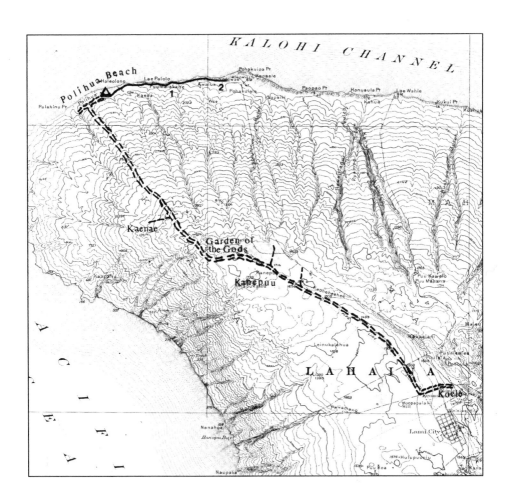

Kukui Nut

23. Kalaupapa

1½ hours down, 2½ hours up
1600 calories; harder
4 miles, round trip
Highest point: 1600 feet
Lowest point: sea level
State Department of Health

The volcanic Kalaupapa Peninsula was formed long after the rest of the Island of Molokai. Jutting out of the otherwise precipitous North Coast of the island, the peninsula is nearly flat except for small Kauhako Crater toward its central portion. The whole peninsula was set aside in the last century for those afflicted with Hansen's Disease (leprosy). With the onset of effective drug therapy, isolation of patients is no longer necessary. As a result, the number of inhabitants of the peninsula steadily diminishes as the patients leave or die.

Though no longer required to stay at Kalaupapa, many patients consider it their home and have chosen to remain in this beautiful area. They enjoy a lifestyle that is even more tranquil than elsewhere in the islands and are most hospitable to visitors. Permission must be obtained to visit Kalaupapa by contacting the State Department of Health. It is best to arrange an escorted tour through Damien Tours (telephone 1-808-567-6171) which will obtain the necessary permission and charges a reasonable fee for an informative tour of the peninsula.

The peninsula may be reached by small plane or by the trail described in this book. The present trail was reputedly built in the early 1900's by a member of the Joao family of Molokai. For many years it was the main route in and out of Kalaupapa, providing access for the mules bringing provisions. It now provides a scenic path for a day hike down the precipitous north cliffs of Molokai to the settlement. It was not the same trail used by Father Damien, the famous priest who aided the people of the settlement in the early years. That trail was

Kalaupapa Peninsula

probably down the steep cliffs farther to the east. Looking at these cliffs, you realize that not the least of the courageous acts of this remarkable man was simply climbing into and out of the settlement.

ROUTE: From the Molokai airport take Highway 46/460 to the junction with Highway 47/470. Turn left onto Highway 47/470 and follow it to the end at Palaau State Park. The park has restrooms, water, and numerous tent campsites in a dense ironwood grove. Permits for overnight camping must be obtained in advance from the Division of State Parks on Maui. At the end of the road in the park, a trail leads to Phallic Rock, a considerable rock formation 400 yards away.

To reach the trailhead, drive out of the park to the first turnoff on the left. This is a short dirt road leading down to the rim of the cliff above Kalaupapa. The trail starts just east of a communications facility at the end of the road. Even though the terrain is steep, the trail is wide. Follow the trail down to the base of the cliff and then along the seacoast to the start of the road to the settlement, where you should be met by your guide. Children under 18 are not permitted in the settlement. Overnight lodgings are unavailable, except at the invitation of the patients.

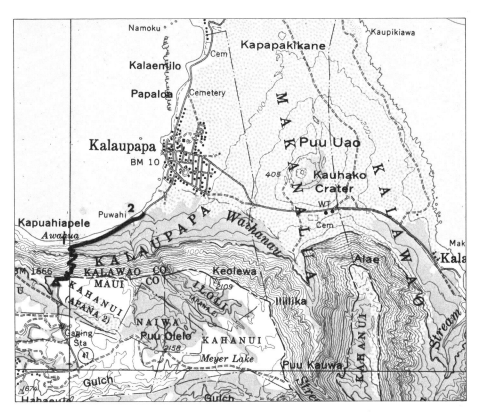

Molokai's North Shore

24. Pepeopae Bog

1° hours
250 calories; easier
1.4 miles, round trip
Highest point: 4150 feet
Lowest point: 3925 feet
The Nature Conservancy of Hawaii

The Pepeopae Bog in the Kamakou Preserve is among the oldest documented bogs in Hawaii, containing an irreplaceable remnant of nature as it was in the Pleistocene Era. The Nature Conservancy of Hawaii protects this extraordinary ecosystem today. A narrow boardwalk, constructed by volunteers, leads through the bog to a lookout platform near its high point. The boardwalk protects the bog and saves the hiker from the muddy slog characteristic of wet Hawaiian trails. Use seed-free footwear with good traction. To learn more about the preserve contact the Nature Conservancy of Hawaii. (See address and phone in introductory section.)

Only a four-wheel-drive vehicle can make the 3/4 to 1-hour-drive on the rough and sometimes confusing dirt road to the trailhead. Do not even think of taking a passenger car. Although no permit is required, contact the preserve manager for updated information on the condition of the road. (See address and phone in introductory section.)

ROUTE: From the west side of Kaunakakai, take Highway 460 westerly. At approximately 3.6 miles turn right (east) onto Molokai Forest Reserve Road, just before coming to a concrete bridge over a dry ravine. Follow the road generally east, as it climbs past former pineapple fields and through lowland covered with imported euvalyptus, silk oak, Cook Island pine and Monterey Cypress. Keep to the main road and ignore numerous turnoffs. The road reaches the Forest Reserve boundary at 5.3 miles from Highway 460 and then soon passes buildings used by Conservancy volunteers. Surrounding areas were reforested in the thirties with exotic species. Migra-

Crossing the bog

tory birds from as far as Alaska may be seen among the thickets.

The road passes a water reservoir at 6.5 miles and skirts Lua Moku Iliahi (the sandalwood measuring pit) at 8.4 miles. At 9.3 miles the trail reaches Waikolu Lookout and picnic area. At this point, stop and enjoy the awesome view of the deep valley and its high waterfalls. The road enters the Kamakou Preserve shortly after passing the

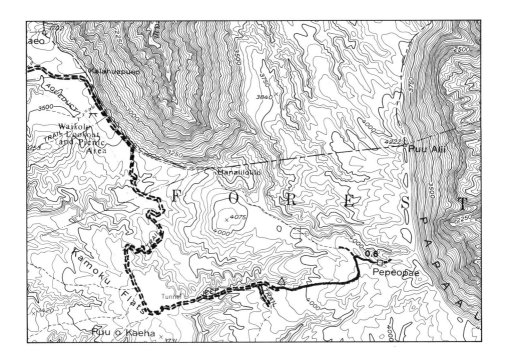

picnic area. Sign in at the box at the entrance. At 9.45 miles the muddy, brushed-over Hanalilolilo Trail enters the road from the left (north). From here the road winds south, crossing over three gulches. Ignore turnoffs to the right, but take the turnoff left at 10.9 miles, which may be signed "Puu Kolekole." At 11.5 milesa left fork in the road leads to the trailhead in 100 yards.

The boardwalk from the trailhead leads gradually uphill into the rain forest. Remain on the boardwalk at all times in this fragile landscape. After about half a mile the trail reaches the cloud-draped bog, with its mosses, sedges, native violets, ancient knee-high ohia lehua trees and lichens strangely reminiscent of Lapland. The outcome of millions of years of isolated evolution remains, pristine. Near the center of the bog the trail turns right, uphill to the observation platform just as the other end of the Hanalilolilo Trail comes in from the left. Retrace your steps to return.

Island of Oahu

Oahu has over 80 percent of the population of the Hawaiian Islands. As might be expected, few of its trails provide a long wilderness hiking experience, such as may be found on Maui, Hawaii, and Kauai. Nevertheless, many day hikes on Oahu are excellent, and can be nicely combined with activities that Honolulu offers. In most cases these trails are accessible by bus for a nominal fare, yet lead through comparatively unpopulated country. All camping, which is quite limited, is by permit from the agency in charge of the area. See the introductory section for addresses and phone numbers to obtain additional information.

Oahu is made up of two mountain areas, the Waianae Range and the Koolau Range, joined by a central plain. The Koolau Range, on the windward side, is twice as long and is covered with much vegetation. On the leeward side is the drier, older, and higher Waianae Range.

In the Waianae Range, the Division of Forestry and Wildlife has recently done admirable work on improving the trails and camping areas and in obtaining access. The

Hibiscus

Kuaokala Trail, the most central, is included here as an introduction to the area. It is a memorable walk through planted groves of pine along the rims of the large valleys of the Waianaes. The Division of Forestry and Wildlife has information on more trails.

The rain-soaked Koolau Range has numerous short and medium length trails, accessible to the public, which lead into its foothills and along its flanks. Most of the Oahu trails described here are in this range. Camping is difficult because the ground is wet and rugged. However, the vegetation in these mountains is lush and varied and there are streams and waterfalls.

The Manana, Waimano, and Mauumae (Lanipo) Trails provide somewhat difficult access to the spine of the Koolau Range, but have quiet and natural beauty that contrasts with the hectic pace of the Honolulu

Windward Oahu from the Pali

Norfolk Island pine grove

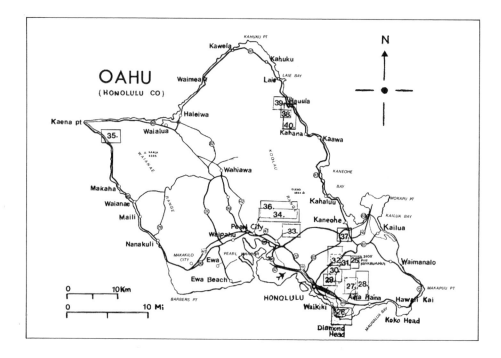

area. The native Hawaiian forest remains largely unspoiled high on the range, where rainfall sometimes exceeds 250 inches a year. There are occasional glimpses of the island and the seacoast through breaks in the clouds. The trade winds sweep the heights steadily and with great force.

Other trails follow the lower spur ridges of the Koolau Range and lead partially up its side valleys. These trails do not reach the rain forest, but give a good taste of nature in Hawaii. These lower elevations have a great variety of plant life, both native and introduced. Here, the newly introduced plants are filling the ecological niches once occupied by native species. The drier portions of this region have thriving eucalyptus and Norfolk Island pine forests. The trails near Hauula on the northeast corner of Oahu and the Aiea Loop Trail above Pearl Harbor lead through such areas.

The well-developed trail complex on Mt. Tantalus, close to Honolulu, is represented by the Manoa Falls, Makiki Valley Loop, Manoa Cliffs, Puu Ohia, and Judd Memorial Trails. After years of work and planning by the Division of Forestry and Wildlife these trails are all interconnected.

They lead through a now-thriving and soil-preserving forest of imported species typical of the reforestation efforts of the early 1900's.

The trail in Diamond Head Crater offers a view of an impressive volcanic crater and the contemporary ruins of the fortress it became. It is also a reminder of the role Hawaii played during the war in the Pacific. Ho'omaluhia Botanical Garden with its trails in windward Oahu, though much influenced by man, is a lovely, quiet place with fine views of the Koolaus.

Crest of the Koolau Range

Jackass Ginger Pool

25. Manoa Falls
2 hours, round trip
450 calories; easier
1.6 miles, round trip
Highest point: 1200 feet
Lowest point: 390 feet
Division of Forestry and Wildlife

The Manoa Falls Trail is the most easily reached of the trails close to Honolulu. The trail is not long, but the dense, rainy forest through which it passes has a great variety of introduced and native plants. Part of the way the trail follows a charming stone footpath through the dense forest. The area's annual rainfall of over 100 inches makes the trail muddy. However, the warm rain at this low elevation should not deter the hiker; the plentiful mosquitoes are less active in the rain. Swimming suits or shorts are probably the best rain gear.

A pool at the base of the falls is big enough for children to wade in. Avoid the pool in high water since rocks may be swept over the falls at these times. Do not climb beyond the falls into the closed watershed. Entry is strictly prohibited by law. Rescue efforts there have led to court appearances and fines. Those with irrepressible energies can make the hard climb to Pauoa Flats up the contouring and zigzagging, but not steep, Aihualoma Trail. Its lower end joins the Manoa Falls Trail shortly before the falls.

ROUTE: Drive up Manoa Road to Paradise Park and Lyon Arboretum near the upper end of Manoa Road in Honolulu's Manoa Valley. Alternatively, take Bus 5, Ala Moana-Manoa, with a Paradise Park sign, to the end of the line at the head of the Manoa Valley. Walk up Manoa Road past Paradise Park and Lyon Arboretum. The road is blocked by a chain barrier fifty yards past Lyon Arboretum, just where a driveway comes up from the wooden houses on the right. The trail starts at the barrier. Go around it and follow the broad dirt path.

The trail leads over a small footbridge across Aihualama Stream and up into the forest reserve. It soon crosses a small stream flowing through a grove of eucalyptus. Beyond the eucalyptus grove, the trail leads along Waihi Stream and passes over the old stone footpath in several places. The trail follows close to the northwest bank of Waihi Stream, but never crosses it. It passes by tangled hau groves, guava, mountain apple, African tulip trees, and ti plants. Toward the end, the trail switchbacks up two small muddy grades before it arrives at the falls.

Manoa Falls Trail

26. Diamond Head
(Point Leahi)

1¼ hours, round trip
300 calories; easier
1.4 miles, round trip
Highest point: 760 feet
Lowest point: 240 feet
Division of State Parks

Diamond Head, well known from posters and postcards, is not only a landmark but also an elaborate World War I and II fortress, which commanded the artillery defenses of leeward Oahu and its strategic ports. Extensive fortifications and tunnels for the fire control areas of the fort were built into the walls of this late Pleistocene tuff (consolidated volcanic ash) cone. These cleverly concealed fortifications are difficult to see from the ground or air and would be costly to attack from the outside of the crater. They can, however, be easily reached by this short trail from the inside. This can be an enjoyable hike for a family because it is short and there is an air of adventure surrounding the old fortifications. However, children must not be allowed to stray off the trail to steep and dangerous areas.

ROUTE: Drive or take the bus to the intersection of Diamond Head Road and 18th Avenue on the northeast side of Diamond Head Crater. The road into the crater begins just west of the intersection. Follow the road 0.7 miles to the tunnel leading into the crater. The tunnel is closed from 6 pm to 6 am. Drive through the tunnel to the parking area where the trailhead is located.

Walk along the wide, paved walkway toward the crater's southwest wall. The trail, bordered by a handrail, soon leaves the flat and winds up to an overlook giving a view of the interior of the crater. The trail then climbs 78 steps leading to a dark, angular tunnel. A flashlight is helpful here, though light is soon visible and the rail acts as a guide through the tunnel. On its far side a steep flight of 99 steps leads into the lowest level of the fire control station which

Crater wall

once commanded the gun batteries on leeward Oahu. From this level a spiral steel staircase of 43 steps leads up to higher levels. The route then leads out through an opening in the fortification onto the last 53 steps up the observation post atop Point Leahi.

The post, the highest point on the rim, commands a view of all leeward Oahu from Koko Head to Waianae. Rainbows and summer breezes now stand watch.

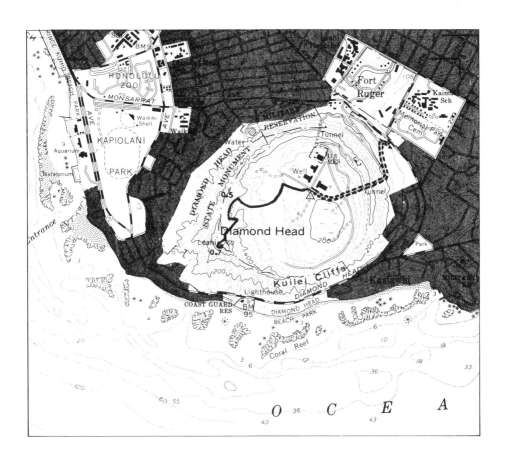

View from Point Leahi

27. Waahila (St. Louis Heights)

3¹/₂ hours, round trip
900 calories; harder
4 miles, round trip
Highest point: 1700 feet
Lowest point: 1020 feet
Division of Forestry and Wildlife

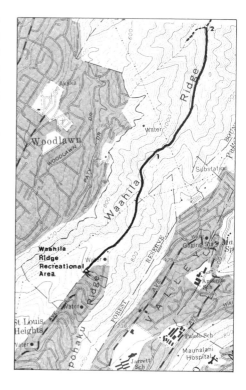

An extensive native forest and spectacular views make this easily accessible trail in the Honolulu area an exceptionally enjoyable day hike. Despite its proximity to the city, the knife-edged ridge that the trail follows assures you that your only company will be fellow hikers. The trail first passes through groves of Norfolk Island pine, ironwood, and guava. It then leads higher to groves of large native koa and ohia trees with dense undergrowth of ferns and large ti plants. The gullies ending against the main ridge support a wide variety of native trees and shrubs. Except for a few minor boulder scrambles which require caution, the trail is generally easy and well maintained. There is no water along the trail. However, there are fountains, eating pavilions, and restrooms in Waahila Ridge State Park at the trailhead. Those choosing to stop for lunch at one of the viewpoints will be pleased to discover that the wind has blown the mosquitoes away to easier pickings in the valleys below.

ROUTE: Drive to the top of St. Louis Heights and turn down Ruth Place to the Waahila Ridge State Park. Parking is available during daylight hours at the uphill end of the recreation area. Alternatively, take Bus 14, St. Louis Heights, to the end of the line on St. Louis Heights and walk down Ruth Place to the state park entrance. Turn uphill to the right just inside the entrance. Follow the broad path uphill paralleling the fenced boundary of the recreation area through a handsome grove of Norfolk Island pine to the parking area.

Several trails lead from the parking area up the ridge, but all soon come together as the ridge narrows. The main trail is centered on the ridge and is broad enough for the first 400 yards to serve as a fire road. Some of the paralleling side trails provide intriguing though confusing tours under canopies of guava and ironwood on deep carpets of needles. About 400 yards from the start, the trail splits just before reaching powerlines crossing over the ridge. One fork continues up the ridge to pass between the two sets of poles on the ridge top. The other drops to the left, passing on the sidehill to the far side of the poles. Both trails quickly rejoin. The trail loses 100 feet of elevation, gains a hundred, loses it, and

Ironwood with Koolau Range in background

False Kamani

then progresses generally uphill along the ridge and under one additional powerline.

At 2.0 miles from the start, the trail splits. The main trail turns left and descends steeply from the ridge through a guava forest resounding with the calls of numerous species of imported birds. At the bottom of this descent, the trail hits a gravelled extension of Alani Drive leading to the Woodlawn area in the Manoa Valley. The righthand branch of the trail continues on up the ridge but should not be taken since it leads to a restricted Honolulu watershed.

28. Mauumae (Lanipo)

5 hours, round trip
1600 calories; harder
6 miles, round trip
Highest point: 2500 feet
Lowest point: 838 feet
Division of Forestry and Wildlife

This steep, challenging trail leads up to a 2,500-foot-high view of windward Oahu, Olomana Peak, Maunawili Valley, and Kaneohe from the top of the Koolau Pali. Since much of the trail goes through a fairly dry part of Oahu, it is especially good for reaching the pali (cliffs) during poor weather. The lower part of the trail passes through generally dry forest and grassy patches which provide good views of Honolulu and the surrounding valleys. There are fine places for secluded picnics. Carry water; none is available on this ridgeline trail.

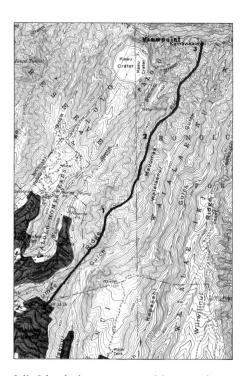

ROUTE: From Waialae Avenue in Kaimuki drive up Wilhelmina Rise and Sierra Drive to Maunalani Circle. Alternatively, take Bus 14 to Maunalani Heights. Go to the highest point on the line, Lurline Drive, and walk to the circle. The trail starts on the Koko Head (east) side of the cyclone-fenced water reservoir area located above Maunalani Circle and passes between two parallel cylcone fences for the first 135 paces. It shortly reaches the spine of the Mauumae Ridge and follows it for the rest of the hike. The ridge dips 200 feet and then climbs steadily all the way to Kainawaanui, a peak on the Koolau Range.

After the initial descent, the trail passes through thickets of staghorn fern, then past large koa trees and ohia lehua. The trail provides one of the few good vantage points of Kaau Crater, an ash and lava cone formed within the last 150,000 years. Kaau Crater is located in closed watershed area No. 1 across Waiomao Stream. Because so few people go into the watershed area, wild pigs may sometimes be seen at a distance on the grass-covered floor of the crater. Nor-

folk Island pine, guava, and ironwood are found along the lower portions of the route. Higher up, the trail passes into a native Hawaiian ohia lehua forest. The trail is steep, rough in some places, and can be slippery after rain. The trail follows the spine of the ridge closely.

False staghorn fern, wawaeiole, swordfern

Mauumae Ridge and the Koolau Range

29. Makiki Valley Loop

2 hours, loop trip
600 calories; easier
2 miles, loop trip
Highest point: 1000 feet
Lowest point: 320 feet
Division of Forestry and Wildlife

The upper Makiki Valley, above Punchbowl, is a lush pocket of tropical forest surrounded by civilization. This forest reserve, the closest to Waikiki and downtown Honolulu, abounds with guava, lilikoi (passion fruit), and mountain apple; yet, only wild pigs and the rare hiker sample their succulent fruits. Numerous species of plants, native and introduced, crowd the area. Small streams sufficient for cooling feet are banked by ginger, taro, and a profusion of flowers. Wild pigs, oblivious to the city a few hundred yards away, quietly roam the forest.

The Makiki Valley Loop is made up of three trails, which form a route up, across, and back down the valley. The Kanealole Trail starts at the Division of Forestry and Wildlife baseyard at the bottom of the valley and leads up to the Makiki Valley Trail, which contours across the valley to join the Maunalaha Trail leading back down to the baseyard.

ROUTE: To reach the Division of Forestry and Wildlife baseyard, go up Makiki Street to Makiki Heights Drive. Follow Makiki Heights Drive about 0.5 miles to the first right turn, where a straight, narrow paved road leads through a state arboretum directly to the baseyard about 400 yards away. The corridor is lined with rows of crimson-flowered African tulip trees and an interesting assortment of other exotic plants, many of which are labeled.

Alternatively, take Bus 15, Pacific Heights, to the intersection of Mott-Smith Drive and Makiki Heights Drive. Walk down Makiki Heights Drive about 0.5 miles to the first left turn, which is the road to the baseyard, and follow it to its end.

Banana plants

Both ends of the loop trail leave from the Division of Forestry and Wildlife baseyard. However, the western trail (the Kanealole Trail) up Kanealole Stream, is the better ascent. This trail is located at the very upper end of the road leading to the baseyard. It follows the course of an abandoned road and is somewhat muddy. About 0.7 miles from its beginning the trail joins the Makiki Valley Trail proceeding across the valley. At this junction the Makiki Valley Trail contours left to Tantalus Drive and right to Round Top Drive. Follow the Makiki Valley Trail right, across the valley, cross-

Makiki Trail

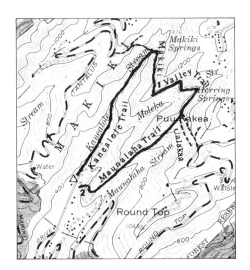

The descent follows a ridgeline for the most part, passing through kukui, eucalyptus, sandalwood, and juniper. The trail passes by interesting rock formations and provides good views of Honolulu. This trail is fairly dry and the switchbacks make the final downhill to the baseyard easy going. The trail crosses a footbridge at the baseyard.

ing Kanealole and Moleka Streams. About 200 paces after the Moleka Stream crossing several trails intersect. The Maunalaha Trail goes down to the right to the baseyard. The Ualakaa Trail leads straight ahead; the Makiki Trail turns left and then contours right to Round Top Drive. To make the loop trip, descend to the baseyard by the Maunalaha Trail.

30. Manoa Cliffs

4 hours, round trip
800 calories; easier
6 miles, round trip
Highest point: 1900 feet
Lowest point: 1400 feet
Division of Forestry and Wildlife

A wide variety of plant life with many species tagged for identification and a thrilling section skirting along the forested cliffs above the Manoa Valley recommend this day hike. Included among the tagged plants are native white hibiscus, kopiko, ohia lehua, kalia, tree fern, mountain apple, mountain naupaka, and koa. These and other species make this trail a favorite field trip for botany students from the nearby University of Hawaii. The trail leads first through ginger, guava, and banana and then onto the cliffs above the Manoa Valley, offering views of the area above Manoa Falls and the whole Manoa Valley. Use caution on the precipitous parts of the trail since the cliffs covered with vegetation are deceptively steep.

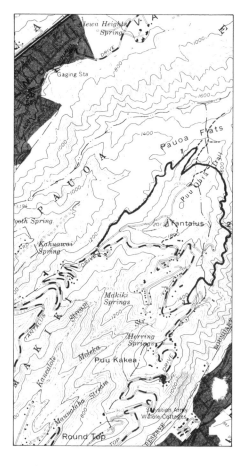

ROUTE: Beginning near the northwest (mountain) side of Punchbowl, drive up Tantalus Drive almost to its top, where Tantalus Drive begins to contour right and a concrete driveway leads straight ahead uphill to the Hawaiian Telephone Company facilities. The trail begins just to the left of this driveway. The trail contours along the northwest side of Tantalus past several small streambeds. About one mile from its start, the trail turns sharply to the right, almost reversing itself, and switchbacks up the hill above Pauoa Flats. Just at this turn, a trail from Pauoa Flats leads in from straight ahead. Care must be exercised to avoid following the trail leading to Pauoa Flats since it may appear to be the main trail. The switchbacks on the Manoa Cliffs Trail lead up through encroaching ginger. Soon the Puu Ohia Trail comes steeply up from Pauoa Flats on the left to join the Manoa Cliffs Trail and leaves again uphill

to the right after about 200 paces. The Manoa Cliffs Trail continues on to contour along the spectacular cliffs above the Manoa Valley. Finally, almost three miles from its start, the trail leads up, right, over a low ridge, and then down to Round Top Drive. You can follow Round Top Drive right, back to the trailhead 1.5 miles away, or return the way you came.

Bamboo grove

31. Puu Ohia (Tantalus)

4 hours, round trip
800 calories; easier
4 miles, round trip
Highest point: 2000 feet
Lowest point: 1580 feet
Division of Forestry and Wildlife

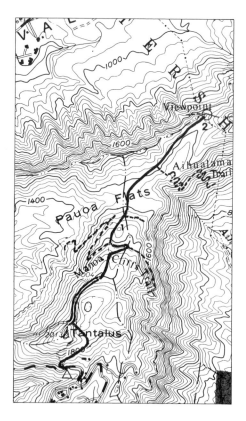

This day hike goes over the top of Puu Ohia (Tantalus), a lush, forested hill with thick bamboo, Norfolk Island pine, and eucalyptus. It eventually leads to a view of the Nuuanu Valley and windward Oahu. A short side trail leads to the small Puu Ohia (Tantalus) Crater. The wide variety of plants, the expansive view at its end, and its proximity to Honolulu and the University of Hawaii make this one of the most heavily traveled trails on Oahu.

ROUTE: The trailhead is opposite a parking area fifty yards west of the highest point on Round Top and Tantalus Drives. Initially the trail switchbacks uphill through guava, ferns, and thickets of bamboo. About 0.5 miles from the start it passes short side trails, one of which leads right, down into Puu Ohia (Tantalus) Crater. Proceed on the main trail, which soon reaches a concrete service road leading up from Tantalus Drive. Follow the road to the right, toward the mountains and to the telephone buildings at the end. The trail continues toward the mountains from directly behind the telephone buildings and heads downhill along a path cut through a thick grove of bamboo. The path soon angles right to join the Manoa Cliffs Trail.

At this junction turn left to follow the Manoa Cliffs Trail for about 200 paces to where the trail to Pauoa Flats leads steeply downhill to a paperbark grove. A confusing array of trails in the grove seems to lead left and right. To get to the lookout above the Nuuanu Valley, continue straight ahead on the well-used trail across the flats, over a maze of exposed and muddy tree roots. The trail veers slightly to the right as it leaves the flats.

It reaches the lookout 0.7 miles after leaving muddy Pauoa Flats, passing the Aihualama Trail on the way. Thick forest of paperbark, bamboo, eucalyptus, and banyan trees darkens the route. Mosquitoes are aggressive, and rain and mud are plentiful. Do not go beyond the lookout into the closed watershed area.

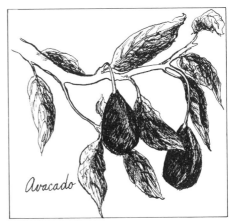

Climbing screwpine (ieie)

Avacado

Nuuanu Valley

32. Judd Memorial (Jackass Ginger Pool)

1 hour, loop trip
250 calories; easiest
1.3 miles, loop trip
Highest point: 700 feet
Lowest point: 680 feet
Division of Forestry and Wildlife

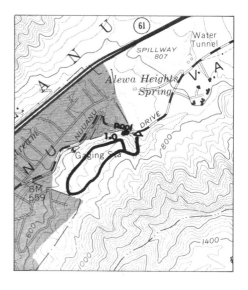

This short trail is ideal for families. In a few places the route is difficult to determine. However, the trail is short, well graded, and passes through pleasant groves of eucalyptus, Norfolk Island pine, and hau trees. Steep, dangerously slippery side trails lead off the main trail.

The trail is named after Charles S. Judd, Territorial Forester from 1914-1939. Judd was one of the foresters of the early 1900's through whose dedication and planning large areas of the Hawaiian Islands were reforested after the thorough and prodigal destruction of the rare native forests by imported livestock. They planted many varieties of imported trees, most noticeably Norfolk Island pine and various species of eucalyptus. The trail passes through an area typical of such a soil-saving reforestation effort. Apart from the hau trees close to the stream course, virtually all the species of vegetation to be seen along the trail are new to Hawaii.

ROUTE: Drive or take Bus 4 up Nuuanu Pali Drive to its stop just before Kimo Drive, shortly before the end of the line. Walk up Nuuanu Pali Drive about 0.7 miles to the downhill side of the short bridge over the Reservoir Two spillway. By car, go up Nuuanu Pali Drive to the Reservoir Two spillway about 0.7 miles past Kimo Drive and just past Poli Hiwa Place. At this point the trail begins, leading directly downhill and east at a right angle to the road. the trail reaches Nuuanu Stream within 50 yards. Rock-hop across the stream and proceed up the far side through a thicket of bamboo, side-hilling up into a grove of turpentine trees. Thereafter the trail rounds a small ridge through a

eucalyptus grove free of underbrush. It then leads into a grove of Norfolk Island pine. The trail has been all but obliterated where it rounds the small ridge, but the trail leading into the Norfolk Island pine grove is well maintained. It contours easily through the Norfolk Island pine to the boundary of the forest reserve where it approaches a residential area near Ragsdale Place. Several confusing side trails lead sharply up or down from the main trail.

At the residential area the trail switchbacks downhill and then begins to return upstream under tangles of hau trees and guava. Within a few minutes walk from the residential area, the trail reaches a bank about 75 feet above Nuuanu Stream. Follow along the bank. Within 3 or 4 minutes after contouring up through a couple of small gullies, the trail forks. One fork leads down a scramble to the swimming

Jackass Ginger Pool

hole, Jackass Ginger Pool (Kahuailanawai). The other fork leads by several routes up the ridge to the trail back.

A clearly apparent alternative trail returns up the far side of Nuuanu Stream from the swimming hole to the highway. Mosquitoes are usually numerous near the swimming hole, especially in shaded areas.

33. Aiea Loop
3 hours, loop trip
800 calories; easier
4.8 miles, loop trip
Highest point: 1600 feet
Lowest point: 700 feet
Division of State Parks

This well-maintained, graded trail passes through a handsome forest. It is a favorite for whole families, from grandparents to small children. About 60 years ago, the area was reforested with Norfolk Island pine, ironwood, brush box, albizzia, and several varieties of eucalyptus. The upper portion of the trail has a covering of native trees and shrubs including ohia lehua, koa, and some sandalwood. In the lower portion the introduced species have replaced the unique Hawaiian species. Since it is located in Keaiwa Heiau State Recreation Area, you can combine the hike with picnics at the park's pavilions or roadside camping (by permit).

The foundation of a *heiau* (temple), formerly used by *kahuna* (Hawaiian priests) practicing medicine, is located at the park and is still in good condition. Labeled examples of medicinal plants used by the kahuna are located near the heiau. At the time of Captain Cook (1778) the kahuna who used such plants were at least as successful in the art of healing as their European counterparts, according to Richard McBride in his book, *Kahuna.* The kahuna had specialists for particular fields of medicine. The heiau at the park was used by the *kahuna la'au lapa'au,* the pharmacologists and general practitioners of the time.

Along the eastern part of the loop is the wreckage of a C-47 cargo plane which crashed in 1943. Parts of the plane are still visible through the dense foliage. The park gates are open only during daylight hours.

ROUTE: Start at Aiea Heights Drive Aiea. Follow it to its end at the park. If traveling by Bus 11, Aiea Heights, get off

Campground

where Kaamilo Road rejoins Aiea Heights and walk about 1.5 miles up Aiea Heights Drive to the well-marked park entrance. The trail starts at the extreme upper end of the main road in the park and leads along the ridgeline, continuing up the ridge steadily until it returns via the ridge to the east. On the trip out, stay on the main trail since several secondary trails lead in and out. The trip along the east ridge gives good views of the Koolau Range to the north and of the surrounding forest.

About two-thirds of the way down the east ridge, the trail passes the wreckage of the C-47, half-buried in a small gully on the right below the trail. Apparently the plane

Aiea Loop Trail

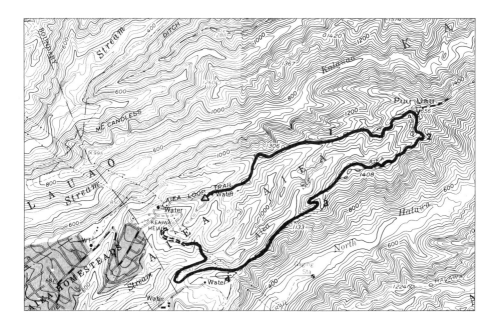

crashed higher on the ridge and over time the wreckage has tumbled down into the small gully. Shortly past the wreck, a side trail, originating at Camp Smith, comes in from the left. The main trail then descends to Aiea Stream, passing through guava and hau trees. It passes under powerlines twice, once on the descent to the stream and again as the trail intersects the stream. The trail then climbs steadily for a short distance along a small gully, past a hau thicket and then into the park camping area next to the road.

34. Waimano

9-10 hours, round trip
1750 calories; hardest
14 miles, round trip
Highest point: 2200 feet
Lowest point: 360 feet
Division of Forestry and Wildlife

This long trail takes you through some of the most lovely country on Oahu, passing a small swimming hole on the way and leading to a spectacular view of windward Oahu from high on the Koolau Pali. The trail provides many good vantage points as it climbs along the cliffsides above Waimano Stream. Unless overgrown beyond the swimming hole, it is possible to follow the trail all the way to the crest of the Koolau Range.

ROUTE: Take H-1 from Honolulu towards Pearl City and turn off at the Waimalu exit to Pearl City. Join Moanalua Road and after a mile turn right onto Waimano Home Road. Follow Waimano Home Road towards the mountains for 2.2 miles to its end at the Waimano Home security fence and guard house. Alternatively, take the Pacific Palisades Bus, to where it leaves Waimano Home Road (Koko Mai Drive) to go to Pacific Palisades. From there walk or take the infrequent Shuttle Bus 71 up Waimano Home Road a mile to the guard house.

The trail begins across from the guardhouse and just before the fence. It splits immediately into an upper and a lower route. Take the upper route, following the fence and the course of an abandoned irrigation ditch and tunnels. The lower, better-maintained route, preferable for the return, follows an old jeep road down to Waimano Stream and eventually climbs steeply to combine with the upper trail about a mile from the trailhead.

Beyond this junction the trail follows the ditch until the ditch ends at a small stream and the remnants of a small diversion dam about 2.5 miles from the trailhead. Cross the stream and turn right. Within a few yards, the trail passes an abandoned irriga-

Windward Oahu from the Pali

tion tunnel through the ridge on the left (north) side of the stream. It soon switchbacks up a short distance to the crest of the ridge.

The trail then follows a cliff edge above Waimano Stream. About 3.3 miles from its start, the trail reaches a dam and pool near the confluence of Waimano Stream and a tributary from the south. At this point the trail crosses Waimano Stream on a small dam and then follows the stream bed up about 30 yards to the confluence of the two streams. It then crosses the left (north) branch and proceeds upstream to follow a course on the ridge between the two branches to the crest of the Koolau Range. The trail beyond is poorly maintained and heavy brush encroaches. Only well-conditioned and experienced hikers should proceed beyond this point. With long pants and sleeves and ample time, the trip is worth taking. This portion of the trail leads through magnificent scenery to a spectacular, windswept viewpoint of windward Oahu from the top of the high Koolau Pali.

The first dam

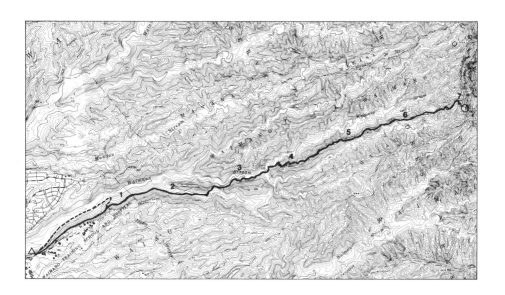

35. Kuaokala

4 hours, round trip
700 calories; harder
5 miles, round trip
Highest point: 1980 feet
Lowest point: 1280 feet
Division of Forestry and Wildlife

The Waianae Range on leeward Oahu offers several forested hiking trails with impressive views. The Kuaokala Trail starts on a paved road and is the most accessible. The Division of Forestry and Wildlife has in recent years done commendable work managing the trails and offers "Na Ala Hele" materials describing the entire trail complex. Road access to the area is limited by a military security checkpoint, but permits for hikers are readily available at the Division of Forestry and Wildlife. There may be hunters so wear bright colors. Guard against fire.

The Waianaes are older and higher than the Koolaus. They are also drier but have deeply eroded valleys and high cliffs. These were formed before the Koolaus arose creating a rain shadow. The Kuaokala Trail winds along the reforested rims of these spectacular "fossil" valleys, formed in wetter times.

ROUTE: After obtaining the permit, drive to the Waianae Coast of Oahu and follow Farrington Highway through Makaha almost to Kaena Point State Park. Just as the park and its beach comes into view, turn uphill to the military security guard station on the right. Present your permit to the guards.

Follow the winding, paved road to the first intersection at the top of the ridge. Turn right and continue for 0.6 miles, passing turnoffs to Kaena Point Tracking Station and up to water tanks. At the second intersection a paved road descends right, steeply into Manini Gulch. The trailhead is on on the right side of that road, close to the intersection. Parking is across from the trailhead.

Grass thriving after fire

The trail climbs through brush to reach the eroded ridgeline, where Southern pine trees, planted by the Division of Forestry and Wildlife in this harsh site begin the long process of restoring the over-grazed land. The trees are infertile clones. This makes it easier to replace them with native species once they have done their work.

The obvious trail, sometimes over eroded ground, by sighing pine or through fragrant, rustling eucalyptus, stays close to the edge of Kuaokala Ridge. It does not descend into the vast, dry valleys below. There are occasional rises and descents until the trail runs into a short spur off of the four-wheel-drive continuation of the road which started into Manini Gulch at the parking area. One may return as one came or by the less interesting dirt road.

A "fossil" valley

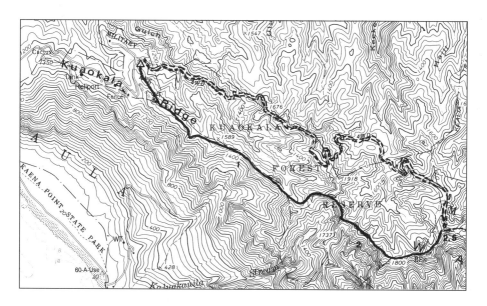

36. Manana
5 hours up, 4 hours down
1800 calories; hardest
12 miles, round trip
Highest point: 2660 feet
Lowest point: 960 feet
Division of Forestry and Wildlife

If you have felt the need to escape from the pressures of population and civilization on Oahu, this is the trail for you. Little used, rough, and not by any stretch of the imagination improved in the upper stretches, it leads into one of the truly wild areas on Oahu. Mud is always plentiful, and in many places brush encroaches on the trail, so suitable clothing must be worn. Hikers should dress for rain since the upper reaches of the trail are in an area that receives up to 200 inches of rain per year. Despite all this, the view and the wilderness at the end of the trail are worth the effort. Only highly experienced hikers should go to the upper portion of the trail. Bright clothing is advisable since there is often pig hunting in the area.

ROUTE: Drive to Waimano Home Road near Pearl City. Proceed mauka (toward the mountains) on Waimano Home Road about 1.2 miles, then left onto Komo Mai Drive to the top of Pacific Palisades. Pass through the Board of Water Supply gate on foot and follow the paved road to the trailhead in the forest reserve, passing under powerlines and by a water tank.

The trail follows a side ridgeline of the Koolau Range all the way to the crest the range. At times the trail may be steep and difficult to follow; avoid trails leading down and off the ridgeline. For example, at about a mile from its start the trail passes an unimproved trail going right and down to the floor of Waimano Valley. The trail may get confusing as the ridgeline nears the spine of the Koolau Range. Carefully note the route for the return trip. Being lost in this area would be a serious matter.

The trail passes first through a forest of eucalyptus trees, bushbox, and guava with a heavy undergrowth of false staghorn fern. Gradually it moves up to areas where native koa, naupaka, lobelia, olapa, and kopiko are found.

If the weather breaks, the Koolau ridgeline provides outstanding views of windward Oahu and Kaneohe Bay. The winds over the Pali are exceptionally strong here. The vegetation high up the trail is typical of the native rain forest. A dense underbrush of ferns, mosses, and shrubs makes for extremely rough going, if you leave the trail. Because of the length of the trail and the roughness of the country, carry a flashlight, food, a map, and a compass. Keep track of the daylight you have left. The sun goes down quickly at this latitude.

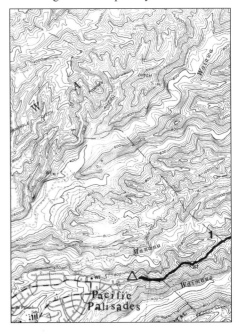

Rain forest

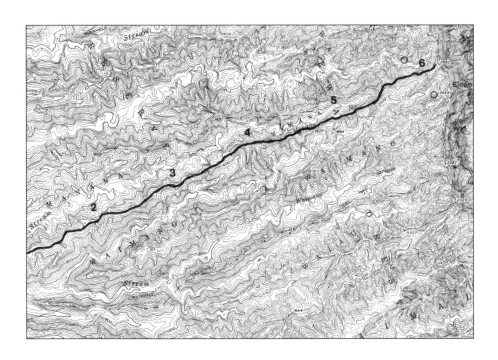

37. Ho'omaluhia Botanical Garden

1 hour, loop trip
250 calories; easiest
2 miles, loop trip
Highest point: 280 feet
Lowest point: 180 feet
Department of Parks and Recreation

Ho'omaluhia, developed in the 1980's as a flood control project in rainy windward Oahu, is one of the four Honolulu Botanical Gardens managed by the Department of Parks and Recreation. The others are Foster, Wahiawa, and Koko Crater. All are worth visiting, but Ho'omaluhia has exhibits, extensive environmental learning programs, guided birdwalks, plant use walks, moonwalks, and nature walks. There are good views up to the Pali and extensive areas for picnics on broad lawns, bordered by a lake.

The nature walks along the park's gentle, waterside paths are scheduled on Saturdays and Sundays. The area is particularly suitable for children, who will enjoy the friendly ducks and fish along the lake shore. Bring mosquito repellant. For more information, contact the Botanical Garden. (See introductory section for address and phone.)

Though the land in the area of Ho'omaluhia is relatively low-lying and flat, it was once part of the great Koolau caldera which reached north to Kaneohe, east to Kailua and south to Waimanalo. Streams and high stands of the sea eroded the landscape, erasing most traces of the caldera, and leaving the 2000-foot-high Pali to the west.

ROUTE: Go to the intersection of the Likelike Highway and the Kamehameha Highway in Kaneohe in Windward Oahu. Go south from the intersection 0.1 miles to Luluku Road, which heads toward the mountains. Follow Luluku Road for a mile to its end at the Ho'omaluhia Garden's Visitor Center. The Visitor Center has displays, slide shows, brochures, and maps of the various paths winding through the garden. Hawaiian plants, palms, and tropical trees from India, Malaysia, Melanesia, Polynesia, and Africa were planted after completion of the earth moving involved in building the flood control dam and lake.

There are many walks that could be taken along the paths in the garden. A favorite loop includes views of the lake and nearby streams. Go from the visitor center down to the lake shore. Then follow around the shore of the peninsula on the southeast side of the lake. Go up along Kamaooalii Stream, then turn away from the stream to join the Pond Trail. Take the Pond Trail back to the lake to complete the loop portion of this route. From the lakeshore retrace your steps to return to the visitor center.

The loop passes by pleasant scenes along the lake and leads into hau thickets characteristic of windward Oahu. Be sure to see the schools of fish that abound in the lake and observe the waterfowl. The view of the Pali from the lakeshore is impressive, even more so after a heavy rain when numerous waterfalls stream down the fluted cliffs. Swimming is not allowed in the lake. The hike can be nicely combined with a picnic.

View of the Pali from Ho'omaluhia

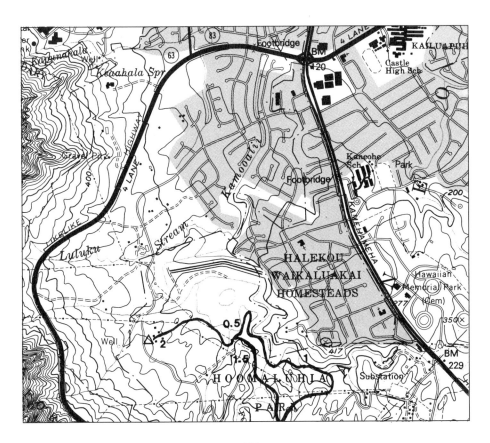

38. Maakua Ridge

2 hours, loop trip
600 calories; easier
2.5 miles, loop trip
Highest point: 650 feet
Lowest point: 40 feet
Division of Forestry and Wildlife

The Maakua Ridge Trail is a pleasant, easy hike traversing a botanical battleground. Legions of the aggressive new arrival, Costa's Curse *(Climedia hirta),* are invading and driving out the plants of the older Hawaiian landscape. In the lower regions Christmas Berry has already won the battle and holds the ground so thickly that tunnels through the brush have been cut for the trail. Hala, ti plants, and ferns typical of Hawaiian landscape before the arrival of the Europeans are still prevalent along the upper portions of the trail.

In the early morning the webs of enterprising spiders lace the trail. The spiders drop quickly to the ground in fright at your approach, except those of a peculiar red and white, crab-like species. Trusting to their armor, these harmless little creatures placidly allow you to approach and photograph them. Their webs, covered with morning dew and always moving in the trade winds, are a beautiful sight.

ROUTE: Drive or take the Circle Island Bus 55 along the Kamehameha Highway (83) to Hauula Beach Park in Hauula. Turn toward the mountains on Hauula Homestead Road, the first road north of Hauula Beach Park. After 0.2 miles, you will reach Maakua Road, just as Hauula Homestead Road veers left. Park by Hauula Homestead Road and walk along Maakua Road about 200 yards until it turns uphill to the right. There the wide, grassy trail leads left, towards the mountains.

In about 125 yards the trail crosses a dry stream bed. About 75 yards after the stream bed the trail comes to a fork. The left fork is the Maakua Gulch Trail, the right fork is the Hauula Loop Trail. Take the left fork to

Trail Tunneling through Christmas Berry

reach the turnoff onto the Maakua Ridge Trail, which starts 150 yards from the junction. The trail immediately crosses the dry bed of Maakua Stream and then switchbacks up the hillside. Part way up, the trail passes the junction with the return leg of the loop, coming in from the left. Continue on, sidehilling toward the mountains, gradually gaining elevation. Ti plants and hala trees come into view.

The trail reaches a ridgeback and climbs fairly steeply for about 200 yards, then drops down into Papali Gulch, located on the southeast side of the main ridge. It

Maakua Gulch

crosses Papali Stream to gain the crest of
the next ridge and switchbacks along its
southeast side. A broad view of the coast
and the sound of the ocean greet you as the
trail rounds the base of the ridge to re-enter
Papali Gulch in deep thickets of Christmas
Berry. The trail switchbacks out of Papali
Gulch and rounds the next ridge to complete
the loop.

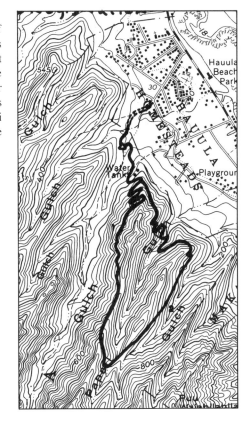

39. Hauula Loop

3 hours, loop trip
500 calories; easier
2.5 miles, loop trip
Highest point: 650 feet
Lowest point: 40 feet
Division of Forestry and Wildlife

The Hauula Loop Trail is one of the three trails on state land near Hauula in windward Oahu. The other two are the Maakua Ridge and Maakua Gulch Trails. The Hauula Trail is the easiest of these trails, since it is well maintained and fairly level. The hike, a gentle loop for the most part, provides good views of the ocean and the nearby settlement of Hauula, passing through groves of planted Norfolk Island pine. Wildflowers and mushrooms grow through the matted needles. The trade winds sweeping over this area have not yet hit the steep, rain-making Pali of the Koolau Range. Thus, the area basks in sun, neighboring the almost perpetual clouds not far inland.

ROUTE: Drive or take the Circle Island Bus 55 on Hwy 83 to Hauula Beach Park in Hauula. Turn toward the mountains on Hauula Homestead Road, which is the first road north of Hauula Beach Park. After 0.2 miles, Hauula Homestead Road reaches Maakua Road, just as Hauula Homestead Road veers left. Park by Hauula Homestead Road and walk along Maakua Road about 200 yards until it turns uphill to the right. There the wide, grassy trail leads left, towards the mountains. In about 125 yards the trail crosses a usually dry stream bed.

The trail comes to a fork about 75 yards after the stream bed. The left fork leads to the Maakua Gulch Trail and further on, to the Maakua Ridge Trail. The right fork is the correct one for the Hauula Loop Trail. About 90 paces from the fork, the Hauula Loop Trail again crosses the usually dry stream bed. It then proceeds on up the side of the ridge, climbing fairly steeply for the first 300 paces. About halfway up the side of the ridge the return portion of the loop comes in from the left (west) to join the trail. Go to the right, switchbacking up the side of the ridge. The trail then contours gently around the ridge, crosses Waipilopilo Gulch, and attains the crest of a second, small ridge. It follows the spine of this second ridge up to a good viewpoint of the upland rain forest at the trail's highest point. The loop trail then descends to recross Waipilopilo Gulch, contours to the crest of the first ridge, and angles down its far side to complete the loop and rejoin the main trail. A scattered few examples of native species of plants are found in Waipilopilo Gulch.

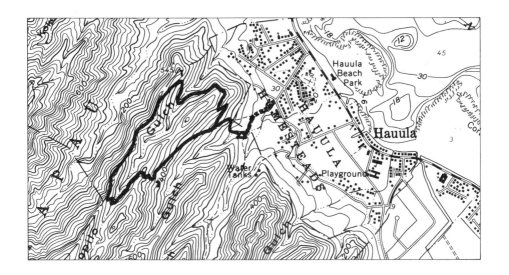

Foothills of Koolau Range

40. Sacred Falls

2¹/₂ hours, round trip
600 calories; easier
4.4 miles, round trip
Highest point: 285 feet
Lowest point: sea level
Division of State Parks

From the heights of the Koolau Range the cool waters of Kaluanui Stream spill delightfully over Sacred Falls, into a deep, boulder-strewn pool. Fern-covered fluted walls rise far above the narrow stream canyon. There is music in the cadence of the plunging waters and the lilt of the stream. The play of shadow and sunlight on the rising cliffs charms the visitor.

The siren beauty of the place obscures a history of danger: flash floods, falling rocks, even robberies. Debris caught high in streamside branches warns of floods filling the canyon from wall to wall. The shattered angularity of rocks in the streambed tells of their deadly fall from canyon walls. Signs, posted by the state because of fatalities, warn hikers of perils along this heavily used trail.

State Parks usually closes the trail during times of flood danger, which is frequent in winter. This is a sensible precaution since in wet weather the danger is greatest. In such weather it is best to pick another day or hike another trail, concluding that it will all still be there.

ROUTE: Drive or take the Circle Island Bus 20 miles north from Kaneohe on the Kamehameha Highway (#83) to Sacred Falls State Park, which is between Punaluu Beach Park and the settlement of Hauula in windward Oahu. The park's large parking area is just north of the bridge over Kaluanui Stream and toward the mountains from Highway 83.

The trail starts toward the mountains from the parking area, where a little-used dirt road passes through a gated cyclone fence. The route follows the dirt road toward the mountains, ignoring turnoffs

Sacred Falls

and generally paralleling the course of Kaluanui Stream. About 1.2 miles from the start the dirt road reaches a grassy area with emergency warning equipment, within a cyclone fence. The trailhead is to the left of the equipment. The trail leads under tangled branches and over a usually dry streambed.

The often muddy trail at first passes through a tunnel of Christmas berry and

124

Mauka—towards the mountains

other exotics. It continues in the direction of the mountains, paralleling the course of Kaluanui Stream. At 0.4 miles from the trailhead, the trail crosses Kaluanui Stream. If the water is high or muddy, do not cross. The canyon can become a trap during flash floods. Even if there is not a drop of rain in the lowlands, floods can still originate upstream in the mountains.

The trail continues up the canyon on the opposite side of the stream as the walls close in. At 0.6 miles from the first crossing the trail comes to a second crossing, where the falls and the end of the trail come into view. The large pool at the base of the falls and water worn boulders occupy the floor of the canyon. Black Malay prawns have made it their home. Beware of falling rocks, especially those within the waterfall. Return as you came.

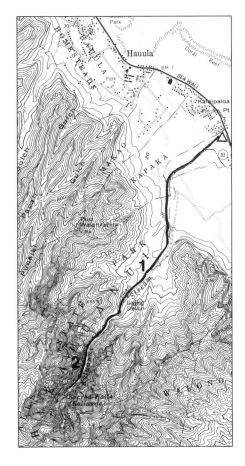

Island of Kauai

Kauai, the early home of Pele, the goddess of volcanism, is the oldest, roughest, and greenest of the Hawaiian Islands. Ever since Pele with her flows of molten lava and showers of volcanic ash left Kauai, erosion has been steadily nibbling at the island with wind, wave, water, and chemical change. This perseverance has produced a land of rare variety and beauty. The towering, fluted cliffs, water falls, and hidden valleys of the Na Pali Coast, deep Waimea Canyon, and the flat, high, and muddy Alakai Swamp are the masterworks of erosion's craft. Into these areas lead the best of the trails on Kauai.

The Canyon Trail winds along the rim of Waimea Canyon, "The Grand Canyon of the Pacific," providing spectacular views. The canyon floor and one of its main side canyons can be reached by taking the Koaie Canyon via Kukui Trail. The floor of Waimea Canyon and of Koaie Canyon offer streams, wilderness camping and views of the ruins of ancient villages. The strenuous journey back up to the canyon rim assures you that there will be few to disturb your solitude on the canyon floor.

The Alakai Swamp, Kawaikoi Stream, Poomau Canyon Vista, and Pihea Trails lead into the high forested plateau country near Kokee State Park. The rustic and suprisingly inexpensive cabins at Kokee State Park, the nearby campground, and the Sugi Grove Campground make good bases for the day hiking trails nearby. These trails lead into fringes of the remote Alakai Swamp and to splendid vantage points of Waimea Canyon and the Na Pali Coast.

The Nualolo-Awaawapuhi Loop Trail descends from Kokee's plateau to the top of the spectacular, unclimbable cliffs above the hanging valleys of the Na Pali Coast.

The famous Kalalau Trail traverses the seacliffs along the rugged Na Pali Coast. It ends at Kalalau Beach where towering cliffs and crashing breakers block all further travel. Wilderness camping, by permit, is available at the beach and intermediate spots along the trail. The Hanakapiai Falls Trail starts two miles down the Kalalau Trail and leads to the falls and pools in an idyllic side valley. Even a partial trip down the Kalalau Trail is rewarding because of the awesome scenery.

Nounou Mountain, the "Sleeping Giant," in the Wailua area presents a tantalizing opportunity. The well-maintained trails can be reached quickly from the nearby populated areas and resorts. The East Side route, described in this book, is one of the three approaches to the top. It offers spectacular views to the seacoast communities and the Wailua River. Hikers climb to its top through a pleasant lowland forest and may get a fine view of the sunset lighting the clouds atop Mt. Waialeale. All this, while the giant slumbers.

Kalalau Valley

Hanakapiai Falls

The Na Pali Coast

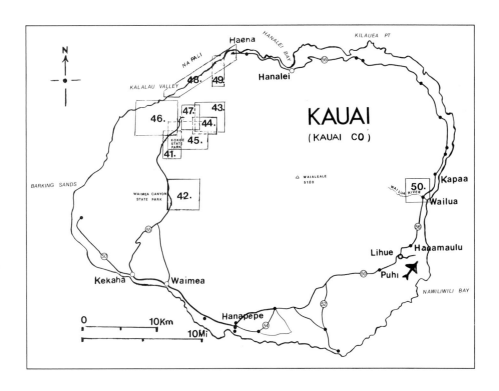

41. Canyon

4 hours, round trip
800 calories; harder
4.8 miles, round trip
Highest point: 3650 feet
Lowest point: 3030 feet
Division of State Parks

A fine view down the length of Waimea Canyon all the way to the sea is the principal attraction of this trail skirting along the Canyon's north rim. A ginger-fringed pool along the route is a pleasant addition. A small waterfall on Kokee Stream spills into the pool across water-smoothed black lava. Along the trail is evidence of the changes taking place in the landscape as native plants are overwhelmed by introduced species, such as, Himalayan blackberry *(Rubus discolor)* and lantana *(Lantana camara)*.

ROUTE: From Kokee State Park Headquarters go 1.3 miles back down Highway 550 towards Waimea to the park entrance sign reading "Kokee State Park." The turnoff is just below the sign, on the east side of the road, towards Waimea Canyon. At the turnoff, a paved driveway leads up to a NASA facility and four-wheel-drive Halemanu Road leads down, left, toward the trailhead. This dirt road is undriveable if wet and, therefore, it is best to park here. The trailhead is only a 0.8-mile walk along Halemanu Road. If you walk the road, add the distance to the trail mileage. The road descends, crosses tiny Halemanu Stream, and at 0.6 miles reaches a turn-off, right, onto an unnamed dirt road. Take this spur road 0.2 miles to its end at a small parking area at the start of the Canyon Trail.

As an alternative, the trailhead can be reached from Kokee Park Headquarters by walking 0.4 miles down Highway 550 to Faye Road, the first dirt road on the left. Follow Faye Road down for 0.4 miles to where it splits right and left. Take the trail, which goes straight ahead (the Unnamed Trail), and follow it for 0.2 miles to

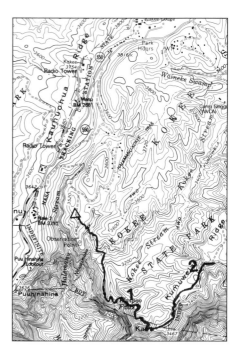

Halemanu Road. At 0.5 miles along Halemanu Road and shortly before coming to Halemanu Stream, an unnamed spur road leads off on the left side of the road. The trailhead is at a small parking area 0.2 miles down the spur road.

The Canyon Trail descends for 50 yards and then splits into two separate trails with the Canyon Trail leading to the left and the Cliff Trail to the right. From the fork the Canyon Trail switchbacks steeply down through remnants of a native koa forest blown down by Hurricane Iwa in 1982. As it reaches the bottom of the first valley it

View down Waimea Canyon

passes above an exposed portion of an irrigation ditch and tunnel system. It then ascends a grass covered hillside and reaches a junction with the Black Pipe Trail coming in from the left at 0.4 miles.

The Canyon Trail leads down onto a broad, bare ridge providing a panoramic vista of the high cliffs of Waimea Canyon to the west and south. In the still, early morning, when the views are best, one may hear the sounds of goats and birds in the distance. Beware the small round rocks on the hard surface, which could roll like ball bearings causing a fatal slip. The trail continues down off the eroded ridge southeast toward the sound of Kokee Stream's Waipoo Falls amid a grove of koa trees in a lush dell at 0.8 miles. A short spur trail leads left, upstream, to the delightful falls and spacious pool surrounded by ginger, koa, ohia, passion flower, kukui, and hala. The main trail continues right, crossing the stream at the top of a smaller, lower falls. It then leads up the grass covered hillside to contour generally east, above the canyon cliffs.

Along the way the trail passes through native koa forests being overwhelmed by blackberry, lantana, and aggressive grass. Silky oak trees and groves of planted Australian eucalyptus seem to hold their own. On this land the ancient plant communities were ravaged by introduced goats. Thus, the soil was exposed to erosion and invasion by introduced plants. These plants have displaced the rare native plants; however, they have the virtue of better withstanding the goats and, thus, saving the soil from erosion.

At about 1.5 miles the trail reaches the ridge overlooking both Waimea and Poomau Canyons. From there one may see the graceful white-tailed tropic birds and flights of dragonfly-like helicopters skirting the cliffs below. The trail levels out as it reaches its end at 2.4 miles on the broad expanse of Kumuwela Lookout at the end of Kumuwela Road.

42. Koaie Canyon via Kukui

2 days; 9 hours, round trip
2600 calories; harder
11 miles, round trip
Highest point: 2925 feet
Lowest point: 650 feet
Division of Forestry and Wildlife

Many view Waimea Canyon, few hike it. The steep Kukui Trail provides the only direct public access to the canyon floor and the Waimea Canyon Trail. The Waimea Canyon Trail leads upstream to a large side canyon, Koaie, and the Koaie Canyon Trail. These trails lead by large, boulder-filled, sometimes flash-flooding mountain streams, bordered by steep canyon walls. It is a strange, empty land, remote from what is expected in Hawaii. Stone walls and house foundations along the trails tell of a vanished people.

The effort involved and the beauty of the warm, dry canyon floor justify an overnight trip. Camping permits from Division of Forestry and Wildlife in Lihue are required. Wear bright clothing because of hunters, be careful of fire, and attempt no stream crossings in high water.

ROUTE: Take Highway 50 west from Lihue to Waimea. Waimea Canyon Drive begins on the right at the Waimea Baptist Church. Follow Waimea Canyon Drive for almost 7 miles to Highway 550. Turn right onto Highway 550 going toward Kokee State Park. The trailhead is on the righthand side a little over two miles from this junction and 6.8 miles down from Kokee State Park.

Walk to the wooden sign-in stand close to the canyon rim, then switchback steeply down a ridgeline toward the Waimea River. The trail reaches a saddle at 1850 feet where the ridge rises out to a small promontory. From the saddle, the trail turns left (north) down an eroded hillside. Near the bottom of the erosion, the trail goes right, into the forest. It switchbacks down ending at Wiliwili Camp shelter on

Canyon wall

the Waimea Canyon Trail near the Waimea River. There are trailside water seeps (treat before drinking) a short way downstream from Wiliwili Camp.

To continue on to Koaie Canyon take the Waimea Canyon Trail upstream. The route may require scrambles along ledges above the river. At about 0.6 miles upstream a fair weather river crossing is located near the foot of Poo Kaeha, a castle-like, volcanic plug on the west side of the river. If the water is low, cross to the

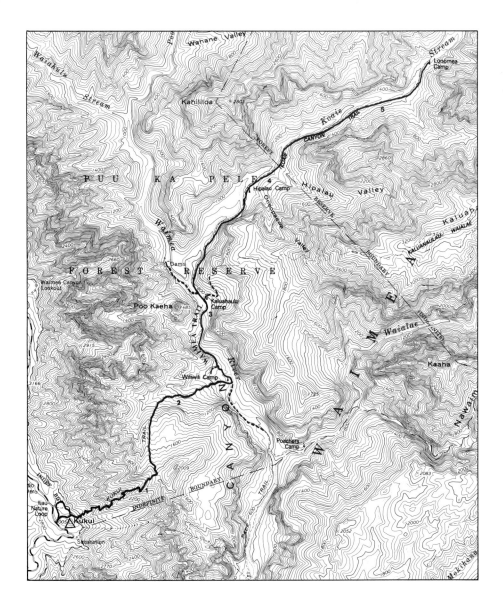

east bank.

Proceed up the east bank of the Waimea River, passing a hunter's shelter at Kaluahaulu Camp. Shortly upstream from the camp the trail passes a turnoff back across the Waimea River, unless obliterated by floods. Continue up the right side, the east bank, of the Waimea River almost to its confluence with Koaie Stream, coming in from the right.

The Koaie Canyon Trail leads up Koaie Canyon, never crossing the stream, through agave plants with their huge sword-shaped leaves and into the forest between the stream and cliffs. The trail passes Hipalau Camp shelter about 0.8 miles up Koaie Canyon. Hipalau Stream, a small, often dry, tributary of Koaie Stream, may wash the trail out in its bed. The trail goes through thickets of kukui trees and guava and passes stone ruins beginning about a mile up Koaie Canyon. The trail ends at about 1.5 miles from Hipalau Camp at Lonomea Camp, an open shelter. Return as you came, best in the cool of the morning.

43. Alakai Swamp

5 hours, round trip
1350 calories; hardest
6.8 miles, round trip
Highest point: 4040 feet
Lowest point: 3700 feet
Division of Forestry and Wildlife

The Alakai is the largest swamp in the Hawaiian Islands, covering about 10 square miles in the center of Kauai. It is almost completely surrounded by cliffs or rugged terrain. In it live some of Hawaii's rarest endemic birds and plants. This desolate area has been comparatively little touched by the outside world. Deep mud and poor forage have protected it from cattle, horses, sheep, and goats, but not, unfortunately, from pigs. All of the swamp lies above the upper limit of mosquitoes' range in Hawaii, about 3000 feet in elevation. Therefore, the endemic birds have been somewhat protected from mosquitoes which may spread diseases.

The Alakai Swamp Trail, skirting just outside the Alakai Wilderness Preserve, provides relatively easy trail access to the north edge of the swamp. It was first laid out to construct a World War II telephone line, little sign of which remains. It ends at Kilohana viewpoint on the rim of the Wainiha Pali. The route is flat and featureless. As a result it may be easy to become lost, especially, since the area is usually exceedingly wet, cloud-covered, and rainy. Some places in the Alakai average 460 inches of rain per year. As a rule it is raining on the trail and the mud is knee deep or worse. It is best to hike the trail only during dry periods.

Greater than usual caution should be exercised to stay on the trail. A compass should be carried and used. Confusing side trails made by hunters and wild pigs lead out periodically. In some areas there are multiple paths leading to the same location made by persons trying to avoid mud holes. If you stray far from trail markers or

Alakai Swamp

the well-trodden path, it is likely that you have gone off the trail. Return to the last known point and start again. You are not lost as long as you know where you came from. The Division of Forestry and Wildlife tries to keep mileage and tape markers along the way and is in the process of building a boardwalk.

ROUTE: From Kokee State Park Headquarters, go 0.1 miles up Highway 550 to Kumuwela Road, a four-wheel-drive dirt road on the right side of the Highway. If wet, which is usually the case, the dirt roads in this area are too slick to be driven, but can be walked as an alternative. As an all weather alternative, take the Pihea Trail

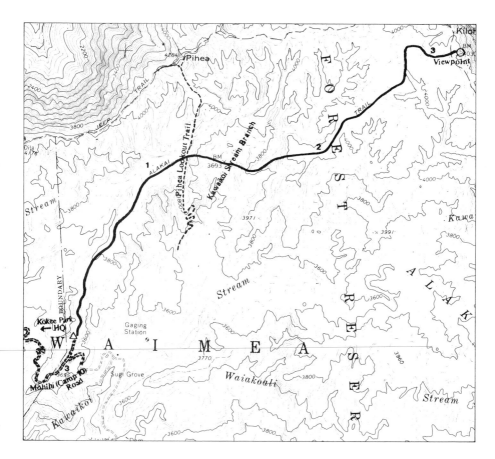

to gain access to the Alakai Swamp Trail. If you walk the roads, add road mileage to trail mileage. Take Kumuwela Road for 1.3 miles to a fork at which Mohihi (Camp 10) Road branches off to the left, ignoring all other turnoffs. At about 1.6 miles Mohihi Road reaches a "4-wheel-drive only" sign, beyond which the road becomes much worse and may be impossible for a vehicle to climb back up. At 3.1 miles from Highway 550, the road comes to the Forest Reserve entrance sign and the Alakai Shelter picnic area. From here a side road leads a little over 0.2 miles, left (north), to a parking area at the trailhead of the Alakai Swamp Trail.

For the first mile the trail follows the remnants of a 4-wheel-drive road used to install the World War II telephone line. The trail passes through the first bog before it crosses the Pihea Trail at 1.3 miles from the trailhead. At approximately 1.5 miles along the trail, after a steep descent of 200 feet in elevation, there is a fair weather crossing of a lovely branch of Kawaikoi Stream. This is a good lunch stop, a turnaround place for the less enthusiastic, and a good place to clean off mud on the return.

The route climbs up from the stream to the open bogs. Mist will quickly cloud camera lenses, and the air is so humid that it may be impossible to dry them off. Photographers should take along several lens filters. At almost three miles from the start, the route veers about 0.2 miles to the left (north). It soon returns to the course it was following and continues on toward the viewpoint at Kilohana, the end of the trail. From Kilohana one can see the Wainiha Valley below and the beaches at Hanalei, provided the weather is clear. The tree-covered Wainiha Valley compares to Waimea Canyon in size, but is seen by few people because of its inaccessibility. The return is made by retracing one's steps.

44. Kawaikoi Stream

1 hour, loop trip
400 calories; easiest
2.5 miles, loop trip
Highest point: 3520 feet
Lowest point: 3440 feet
Division of Forestry and Wildlife

This nearly level trail follows along the banks of remote and lovely Kawaikoi Stream, one of the principal streams draining the Alakai Swamp. It is the habitat for many of the swamp's rare water fowl. These may be photographed with a telephoto lens, if approached quietly. The tannin from the luxuriant vegetation through which the stream flows stains its waters the color of tea.

ROUTE: From Kokee State Park Headquarters go 0.1 miles up Highway 550 to Kumuwela Road, a four-wheel-drive dirt road on the right side of the Highway. If wet, the dirt roads in this area are too slick to be driven, but can be walked as an alternative. If you walk the roads, add road mileage to trail mileage. Measure road mileage from the start of Kumuwela Road. Ignoring all previous turnoffs, take this dirt road for approximately 1.3 miles to a fork at which Mohihi (Camp 10) Road branches off to the left. Follow Mohihi Road, which reaches a "4-wheel-drive only" sign at 1.6 miles from the Highway. Beyond this sign the road gets much worse.

Follow Mohihi Road until you are 3.7 miles from the Highway. At this point you will reach Kawaikoi Camp and Picnic Area and a dry weather ford across Kawaikoi Stream. The trailhead is 100 yards beyond the ford, on the left, across from Sugi Grove Camp. The trail starts in a dense, vigorous grove of Japanese sugi (cedar) and redwoods planted during the Great Depression. It soon nears the stream and continues east along the south (right) bank.

At about 0.7 miles from its start the trail passes by a ford to the Pihea Trail. The Kawaikoi Stream Trail does not cross the

Blackberry

ford, but continues up on the south bank. At 0.8 miles the trail starts a loop, with the right hand branch sidehilling east away from the stream. It soon returns, continuing upstream atop a 40 foot bluff. The trail descends and makes a sharp left turn to a dry weather crossing near the bluff. After this crossing the trail turns back downstream on the opposite side. It closely follows the stream on slippery footing to a dry weather crossing back across the stream, completing the loop. Follow the trail back downstream to return to the trailhead.

Sugi Grove Campground, 0.1 miles further down Mohihi Road from the trailhead, is a quiet, streamside camping area in a dense grove of large sugi trees. It may be crowded during fishing season in August or September. Since the Kawaikoi Stream Trail is only a day hike, Sugi Grove, Kawaikoi Camp, and Kokee State Park Campgrounds are good spots for overnight camping in connection with hikes on this trail.

Kawaikoi Stream

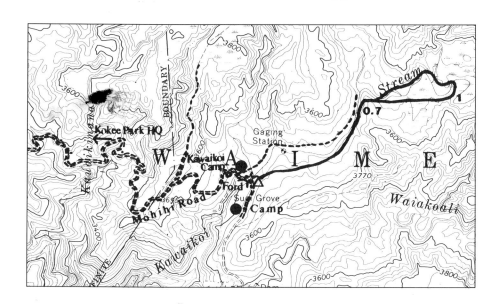

45. Poomau Canyon Vista

¹/₂ hour, round trip
100 calories; easiest
0.6 miles, round trip
Highest point: 3500 feet
Lowest point: 3400 feet
Divison of Forestry and Wildlife

The sheer cliffs of Poomau Canyon, though most impressive, are rarely seen by visitors since one must walk to see them. Most people view Waimea Canyon from the lookouts on Highway 550 and leave it at that. The Poomau Canyon Vista Trail provides an additional vantage point for those wishing to see more.

ROUTE: From Kokee State Park Headquarters go up 0.1 miles on Highway 550 to Kumuwela Road, a four-wheel-drive dirt road on the right side of the Highway. If wet, the dirt roads in this area are too slick to be driven, but can be walked as an alternative. If you walk the roads, add road mileage to trail mileage. Measure road mileage from the start of Kumuwela Road. Take Kumuwela Road for 1.3 miles to a fork at which Mohihi (Camp 10) Road branches off to the left, ignoring all other turnoffs. Follow Mohihi Road, which reaches a "4-wheel-drive only" sign at 1.6 miles. Beyond this sign the road becomes much worse and may be too slick for a vehicle to climb back up.

At 3.7 miles from the Highway, Mohihi Road reaches Kawaikoi Camp and Picnic Area and a dry weather ford across Kawaikoi Stream. After crossing Kawaikoi Stream, the road leads past Sugi Grove, a quiet campground adjacent to the stream in a stand of tall Japanese sugi trees.

The Poomau Canyon Vista Trail trailhead is about 0.8 miles beyond the Kawaikoi Stream crossing and 4.6 miles from the Highway, shortly after the road crosses Waiakoali Stream. The trail leads off to the right of a 40-foot-high Norfolk Island Pine. It goes through a stand of sugi trees, across a small footbridge over an

Trailhead and Norfolk Island Pine

irrigation ditch paralleled by a dirt ditch road, and then into the native upland forest. It passes a wide variety of endemic plants, as it switchbacks down to the viewpoint above Poomau Canyon. From there you may see a great distance down the length of Poomau and Waimea Canyons and watch the graceful white-tailed tropic birds gliding on the winds near the cliffs below. Photography is best in early morning or late afternoon.

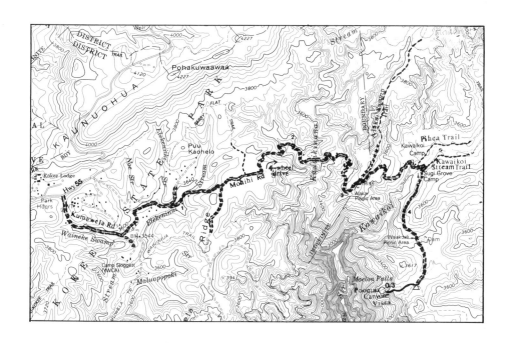

Poomau Canyon Vista

46. Nualolo-Awaawapuhi Loop

7 hours, loop trip
2300 calories; harder
9.5 miles, loop trip
Highest point: 3800 feet
Lowest point: 2234 feet
Division of Forestry and Wildlife

Views of endemic Hawaiian forest and the awesome cliffs above the isolated hanging valleys on the Na Pali Coast are the rewards for the substantial effort required on this loop route. The upper portions of the loop pass through the Kuia Natural Area Reserve before the trees thin out as the trails pass through drier, more open areas near the tops of the great fluted cliffs of the Na Pali Coast. In places the loop is steep, deeply rutted, or dangerously exposed. It may be muddy and slippery, especially in some of the steeper areas. Either leg of the loop can be hiked separately. For a shorter trip go and return on the Awaawapuhi leg of the loop.

Be careful of hunters and the small round rocks which make for treacherous footing on eroded cliff rims. Carry flashlights. The plants in the native dryland forest are rare and the danger of fires extreme; thus, neither overnight camping nor fires are permitted. Water is unavailable.

ROUTE: The Nualolo Trail begins on Highway 550, just below Kokee State Park Headquarters, which is near Kokee Lodge. The trail starts up sharply for about 400 yards and then leads generally downhill and northwesterly through dense forest and over occasional grassy areas. A little over 1.5 miles from its start the trail curves to the left. The trail continues generally northwestward and downhill through drier and drier forest.

At about the 3-mile mark the trail splits. Follow the right fork, which leads down a steep incline. At about 3.2 miles, near the bottom of the steep incline, the Nualolo Cliff Trail goes out to the right.

Hikers may continue on the Nualolo Trail for about half a mile, going generally downhill through open country to the bench land on the south rim of the Nualolo Valley. The trail follows the rim until it officially ends at a U.S.G.S. survey marker titled "Lolo No. 2," and offers a spectacular viewpoint.

Return to the Nualolo Cliff Trail, which is a connector trail, to make the loop trip with the Awaawapuhi Trail. The Nualolo Cliff Trail contours for two miles before reaching the Awaawapuhi Trail. Along the way there are some narrow spots at cliff's edge. However, it passes spectacular scenery and also a Division of Forestry and Wildlife picnic shelter. Turn left at the well-travelled Awaawapuhi Trail. In about half a mile there is another spectacular viewpoint at the metal railings marking the trail's end.

Allow some time to enjoy the views to the sea, the fluted cliffs, white-tailed tropic birds, and the inevitable 8 a.m. helicopters. Return up the Awaawapuhi Trail to the junction with Nualolo Cliff Trail. Then continue up, switchbacking for 2.8 miles until reaching the highway.

Along the way the Division of Forestry and Wildlife has marked many endemic plants, for which it has published an interpretive guide available at the Division's office in Lihue or at the Kokee Museum. The trail ends at about 1.7 miles up the road from Kokee Lodge and Park Headquaters near the 17-mile marker on Highway 550. Be careful of cars when walking along the shoulderless highway to return to Park Headquarters.

Helicopter venturing among the Na Pali Cliffs

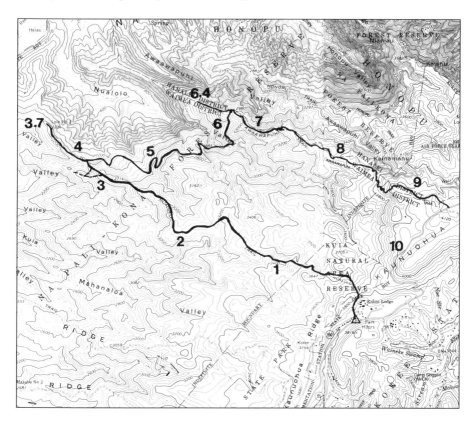

47. Pihea

5-6 hours, round trip
1100 calories; harder
7 miles, round trip
Highest point: 4284 feet
Lowest point: 3420 feet
Division of Forestry and Wildlife

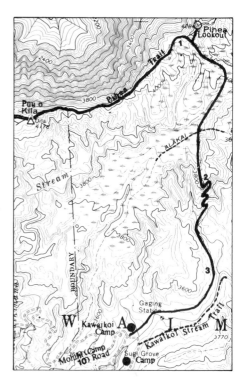

Skirting the great fluted cliffs above the Kalalau Valley, and ending along Kawaikoi Stream, the Pihea Trail provides some of the best scenery in the Hawaiian Islands. It borders the expanse of the Alakai Swamp and provides all-weather access to the Alakai Swamp Trail. The trail is most pleasant early in the morning, when you have a good chance of seeing many native Hawaiian birds feeding in the trees along the trail and goats clambering with remarkable aplomb along the precipitous cliffs below.

The ocean and sky provide an immense backdrop of varying shades of blue and white. The light of the rising sun playing on the fluted cliffs offers exceptionally good color for photos. Ohia lehua trees with their brilliant red flowers, ferns of various sorts, mosses, and white lichens are found along the trail.

ROUTE: Take Highway 50 west from Lihue almost all the way through Waimea to Waimea Canyon Drive, beginning on the right at the Waimea Baptist Church, Follow Waimea Canyon Drive for almost 7 miles to Highway 55. Turn right onto Highway 55 and follow it past Kokee State Park, Kokee Air Force Station, and the Kalalau Lookout to the very end of the paved road at the Puu O Kila Lookout.

The trail begins at the lookout, following the remnants of a road-building attempt along the edge of the cliffs above the Kalalau Valley. Fortunately people thought better of it and work on this desecration was stopped. However, erosion started by the road cuts continues, and it is only a matter of time before the narrow ridge itself will be bisected. As the trail approaches the Alakai Swamp the vegetation becomes

more luxuriant. After 1.1 miles a spur leads up a short distance to the Pihea Lookout.

The main trail descends southerly, skirting the bogs of the Alakai Swamp. At about 1.7 miles the trail crosses the Alakai Swamp Trail in a flat, swampy area crowded with small trees. It then makes a switchbacking descent to branches of Kawaikoi Stream. At about 3.3 miles, after crossing a small stream, the trail passes by a fair-weather ford leading across Kawaikoi Stream to the Kawaikoi Stream Trail. The Pihea Trail continues down the northwest side of Kawaikoi Stream half a mile to end at the

Pali above Kalalau Valley

Mohihi Road (Camp 10 Road).

Good overnight tent camping (by permit)
is available at nearby Kokee State Park and
Sugi Grove Campground. To use the cabins
at Kokee State Park, make reservations well
in advance.

48. Kalalau Trail

2-4 days; 18 hours, round trip
4900 calories; hardest
22 miles, round trip
Highest point: 800 feet
Lowest point: sea level
Division of State Parks

Many would say that this is the best of all Hawaiian trails because of the dry, balmy weather, massive, fluted cliffs, and the delightful, isolated beaches found along the route. The Na Pali Coast which it follows is one of the oldest portions of the Hawaiian Islands. It has been heavily eroded by the elements, forming spectacular cliffs and valleys along its entire length. The trail with modern improvements, follows the course of an ancient Hawaiian trail, parts of which are still visible.

Obtain permits for camping and for day use beyond Hanakapiai from the Division of State Parks in Lihue (open weekdays only). Boots are necessary on the trail, particularly beyond Hanakoa, because of dangerous washouts.

ROUTE: Take Highway 56 north to its very end, on the North Shore at Kee Beach, past Hanalei, about 38 miles from Lihue. The trail begins at a sign-in stand left of the parking lot. Several springs and streams,

about an hour apart, provide treatable water along this trail. About 2 miles from the trailhead, the trail reaches the Hanakapiai Valley. At the mouth of the valley, there is a sandy beach of exceptional beauty. (The Hanakapiai Falls Trail, leading to the falls in the valley, starts where the Kalalau Trail crosses Hanakapiai Stream.) Beyond the stream, the Kalalau Trail climbs steeply, crossing the Hoolulu and Waiahuakua Valleys before reaching the Hanakoa Valley, midway on this long trail. In summer,

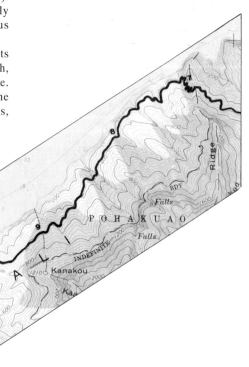

guava and mountain apple are plentiful along this trail. There is much evidence of taro cultivation in earlier times.

At 6.0 miles, the trail reaches Hanakoa Shack, a shelter available to hikers. Camping sites are located nearby and water is plentiful. A short path leads from the front of the shelter to Hanakoa Pool, a delightful swimming hole in Hanakoa Stream. Just beyond the stream, a short side trail leads upstream to the falls.

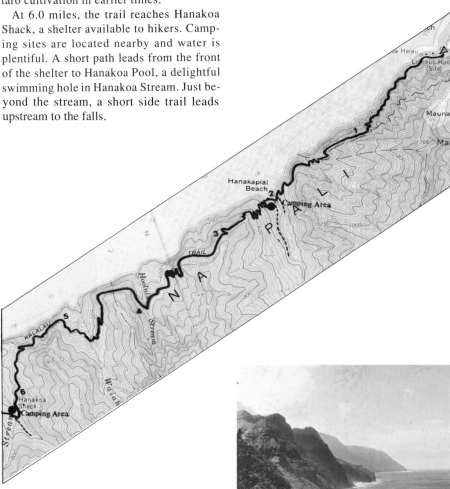

About 9.5 miles from the start, the trail begins to descend the east slope of the Kalalau Valley to the beach, past numerous stone walls and former taro patches. The last of these patches was abandoned by the twenties.

Proceed along one of the paths paralleling the beach. The permitted camping area is just inland, toward the west end of the beach. Treatable water is available from the cascading part of a small waterfall located at the west end of the beach.

The Na Pali Coast

Strong currents along the Na Pali Coast have caused drownings. In places this long trail can be frighteningly narrow and exposed or slippery when wet. Nonetheless, even a short hike to the first viewpoints is rewarding. The hike all the way to Kalalau Beach and back is incomparable.

49. Hanakapiai Falls via Kalalau Trail

5-6 hours, round trip
1500 calories; harder
7 miles, round trip
Highest point: 800 feet
Lowest point: 40 feet
Division of State Parks

This lovely trail leads into a sheltered valley, once thickly settled. Now only scattered, abandoned taro patches, stone walls, and house foundations remain as evidence of the once-thriving agricultural population. From ancient times the fertility of the soil and the abundance of water made the valley well suited for taro production. Later, cash crops were raised. However, since the area was small and far from the markets, such enterprises proved unprofitable. The trail passes the ruins of a small coffee mill which used Hanakapiai Stream as its power source. Little remains except a large stone chimney.

Cattle raising was attempted after the people left the valley, but this proved so destructive to the land that the cattle were finally removed and the land was placed under state administration. In this status it has been gradually recovering for the last half century. The scattered descendants of the various cultivated plants now richly cover the valley floor. An occasional taro plant grows haphazardly next to kukui trees. Guava and mango offer their succulent fruit to passersby, and the worst of man's abuses are slowly being erased.

ROUTE: The Hanakapiai Falls Trail branches off the Kalalau Trail. To reach the Kalalau Trail, follow the directions under that heading. The head of the Hanakapiai Valley Trail is marked by a large sign about 2 miles from the beginning of the Kalalau Trail and shortly after it crosses Hanakapiai Stream. The trail leads up the west bank of Hanakapiai Stream and is fairly easy for about a mile. It passes close by the coffee mill ruins toward the beginning of the trail. Further on, the route becomes increasingly difficult and crosses to the other side of the

Monstera

stream.

The trail leads by a series of lovely, small waterfalls and pools and ultimately ends at the main waterfall. There, a broad, deep pool formed by the falls provides ample room for a refreshing swim. Large stones surrounding the pool make fine perches for sunbathing.

Stream crossing points and the trail itself are subject to change because of changes in the stream and use of the trail. The trail is not well defined at this time. However, if you follow the main stream, you will not go far wrong. If the stream is flooding, it is best not to continue since the upper crossings become progressively more difficult. When swimming in the pool below the main falls, beware of rocks swept down in the falls, especially during high water. Strong currents may make the beach unsafe for swimming.

Hanakapiai Beach

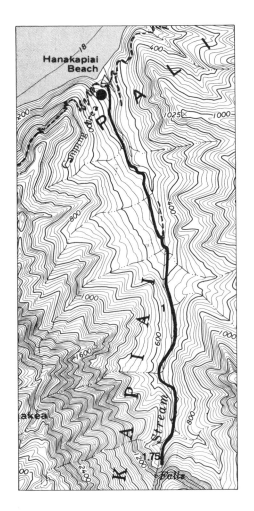

50. Nounou Mountain via East Side

3-4 hours, round trip
600 calories; harder
3.5 miles, round trip
Highest point: 1120 feet
Lowest point: 120 feet
Division of Forestry and Wildlife

Nounou mountain is an extraordinarily inviting landmark. According to popular folklore the mountain is the body of a sleeping giant, turned to stone. Viewed from the mouth of the Wailea River, the skyline of the mountain does give support to such a theory. Imagination gives rise to the almost irresistible impulse to walk atop the sleeping giant, always with a slight fear that he might awake in irritation.

Besides this, from the top of Nounou Mountain the setting sun, playing up through Mt. Waialeale's ever-present clouds, can present scenes of splendor and infinite variety. The shelter atop Nounou Mountain at the end of this trail provides a fine viewpoint of the sunset. In the evening the open hillside on the way back offers good views of the changing light. Night falls so quickly in Hawaii that, if hikers wait until sunset to start down, flashlights and care to avoid drop-offs will be necessary for the return trip. There are no campsites in the Nounou Forest Reserve.

ROUTE: Drive north from Lihue on Highway 56 for 6.0 miles to Haleilio Road, which is on the left, about 0.4 miles past the bridge over the Wailua River. Turn left onto Haleilio Road toward Nounou Mountain and drive for one mile until Haleilio Road curves left near telephone pole no. 38. Take the blacktopped driveway on the right leading uphill to the Department of Water pump site. The trailhead is on the left, just before the pumping equipment.

The trail starts first among trees but soon leaves them and switchbacks up the broad brush and grass-covered hillside. After a little over 0.5 miles, as the hillside

Cliffside view of the Wailua River

become steeper, the trail comes to the cliff's edge on the south side of the slope. Here a side path leads steeply up along the edge, seemingly providing a direct route to the top. Avoid it. It leads to dangerous, steep ledges of crumbling rock.

The correct route switchbacks to the right, north, across the slope, descending before it switchbacks up again through woods well to the northern slope. Eventually, it skirts cliffs and eroded areas of red soil, perils to returning hikers hurrying down in the dark, and leads west until it is joined by the trail coming in from the west.

The trail continues to climb turning southerly ending at the shelter atop the Sleeping Giant. An unofficial trail, somewhat steep and exposed to cliffs, continues on from the shelter clearing in a scramble onto the giant's head. Be sure to return before dark.

View of the Sleeping Giant across the Wailua River

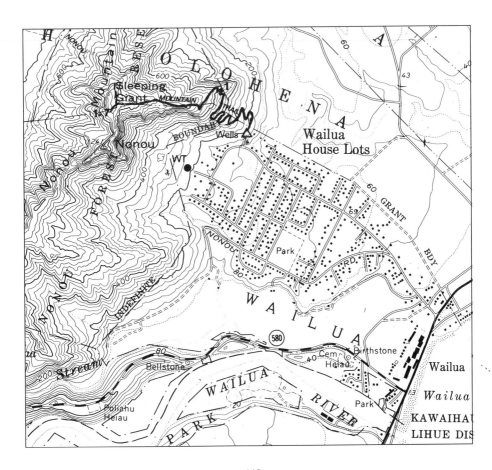

Index